A Treatment for Adolescents Displaying Harmful Sexual Behaviour *of related interest*

Children Who Commit Acts of Serious Interpersonal Violence
Messages for Best Practice
Edited by Ann Hagell and Renuka Jeyarajah-Dent
ISBN 978 1 84310 384 4

Boys Who Have Abused
Psychoanalytic Psychotherapy with Victim/Perpetrators of Sexual Abuse
John Woods
Foreword by Arnon Bentovim
With a contribution from Anne Alvarez
ISBN 978 1 84310 093 5
Forensic Focus Series

Conduct Disorder and Offending Behaviour in Young People
Findings from Research
Kristin Liabø and Joanna Richardson
ISBN 978 1 84310 508 4
Child and Adolescent Mental Health Series

Sexual Offending and Mental Health
Multidisciplinary Management in the Community
Edited by Julia Houston and Sarah Galloway
Foreword by Dawn Fisher
ISBN 978 1 84310 550 3
Forensic Focus Series

Managing Men Who Sexually Abuse
David Briggs and Roger Kennington
ISBN 978 1 85302 807 6

What Have I Done?
A Victim Empathy Programme for Young People
Pete Wallis with Clair Aldington and Marian Liebmann
ISBN 978 1 84310 979 2

Disability and Child Sexual Abuse
Lessons from Survivors' Narratives for Effective Protection, Prevention and Treatment
Martina Higgins and John Swain
ISBN 978 1 84310 563 3

A Treatment Manual
for Adolescents Displaying Harmful Sexual Behaviour

Change for Good

Eamon McCrory

Illustrated by Paula Walker-Rhymes

Jessica Kingsley *Publishers*
London and Philadelphia

First published in 2011
by Jessica Kingsley Publishers
116 Pentonville Road
London N1 9JB, UK
and
400 Market Street, Suite 400
Philadelphia, PA 19106, USA

www.jkp.com

Copyright © Eamon McCrory 2011
Illustrations copyright © Paula Rhymes 2011
Foreword copyright © Jon Brown 2011
All illustrations in the Character Library are the work of Paula Rhymes (paula.walkerrhymes@talktalk.net). In addition, the illustrations on pp. 36–7, pp. 70–77, p.84, p.86, p.87, p.107, p.155 and p.279 of the CD-Rom include figures and background scenes from the Character Library by Paula Rhymes. The Sexual Fact Sheet illustrations on pp. 250–254 are by Lucinda Shoolbred. All other illustrations and figures are by Eamon McCrory.

All rights reserved. No part of this publication may be reproduced in any material form (including photocopying or storing it in any medium by electronic means and whether or not transiently or incidentally to some other use of this publication) without the written permission of the copyright owner except in accordance with the provisions of the Copyright, Designs and Patents Act 1988 or under the terms of a licence issued by the Copyright Licensing Agency Ltd, Saffron House, 6–10 Kirby Street, London EC1N 8TS. Applications for the copyright owner's written permission to reproduce any part of this publication should be addressed to the publisher.

End User Licence Agreement for the CD-ROM
Jessica Kingsley Publishers is granting you, as the purchaser of the CD-ROM accompanying this resource, a non-transferable licence to use and print the files and images on the CD-ROM for use in a professional context; however, you may not use this work for personal use or for commercial purposes unless you have been granted permission from the publisher. Copying and distribution of the entire work or sections of the work is also prohibited. Full details of the licence granted are provided on the accompanying CD-ROM. This does not affect your fair use and other rights.

Warning: The doing of an unauthorised act in relation to a copyright work may result in both a civil claim for damages and criminal prosecution.

Library of Congress Cataloging in Publication Data
McCrory, Eamon.
 A treatment manual for adolescents displaying harmful sexual behaviour : change for good / Eamon McCrory ; illustrated by Paula Walker-Rhymes.
   p. cm.
 Includes bibliographical references.
 ISBN 978-1-84905-146-0 (alk. paper)
 1. Teenage sex offenders. 2. Teenage sex offenders--Rehabilitation.
3. Teenagers--Sexual behavior. 4. Sex crimes--Prevention. I. Title.
 HV9067.S48M336 2010
 616.85'830651--dc22
                  2010020521

British Library Cataloguing in Publication Data
A CIP catalogue record for this book is available from the British Library

ISBN 978 1 84905 146 0

Printed and bound in Great Britain by
MPG Books Group

Acknowledgements

Creating this treatment manual for adolescents displaying harmful sexual behaviour – the *Change for Good* manual – has been a collaborative exercise that has drawn together the skills, expertise and experience of many individuals. It has been funded by the NSPCC and developed in the context of the clinical work conducted in the NSPCC's National Clinical Assessment and Treatment Service (NCATS) in London. NCATS (previously known as YAP) is a multidisciplinary team with psychology, social work, psychiatry and psychotherapy professionals working together to assess and treat a wide range of children and adolescents presenting with harmful sexual behaviour.

The manual builds on and advances many years of previous clinical experience with this client group, including a CBT group programme run by the NCATS clinical service. We owe a debt to each of the many young people we have been able to help over the years and to our NCATS colleagues who have made a valued contribution to this manual. We wish to thank Colin Hawkes, Judith Usiskin, Susan Haacke, Andrew Azzopardi, Hilary Crew and Richard Reynolds for their help. Beyond our own team we have been very grateful for the valuable input from a variety of professional colleagues, including Jackie Craissati, Lesley French, Sheena Webb and Marcus Erooga, as well as the input from colleagues from other NSPCC teams. The manual has benefited in many ways from the thoughtful suggestions and attention to detail they have generously provided. On a much broader level we are indebted to the many researchers and clinicians whose contributions have had an international influence on practice and which have set the context for this manual.

We also want to acknowledge the generous support of the NSPCC, and in particular Lorraine Radford (Head of NSPCC Research) who commissioned the work in the first place. Together with Lindsey Calpin (Assistant Director, NSPCC Fresh Start), they have ensured that work on developing this manual has been fully supported at every stage. William Baginsky (Head of Child Protection Learning Resources, NSPCC) deserves special thanks for his patience and tireless efforts over the last two years in helping to transform our clinical ideas into a published and accessible form.

Author and Contributors

AUTHOR

Eamon McCrory is a consultant clinical psychologist with the NSPCC based at the National Clinical Assessment and Treatment Service (NCATS) in London. He is a senior lecturer at UCL where he co-directs the Developmental Risk and Resilience Unit and is Head of Postgraduate Studies at the Anna Freud Centre. His research and clinical interests have focused on conduct problems in childhood and more recently on the neuroscience of early adversity. He is currently completing a three-year study using functional magnetic brain imaging to investigate emotion processing and identify neural markers of resilience following childhood maltreatment.

CONTRIBUTING AUTHORS

Sam Blackburn is a research psychologist with the NSPCC's National Clinical Assessment and Treatment Service (NCATS).

Dr Elly Farmer is a clinical psychologist with the NSPCC's National Clinical Assessment and Treatment Service (NCATS).

Dr Peter Fuggle is a consultant clinical psychologist for Islington Primary Care Trust.

Dr Lucinda Shoolbred is a clinical psychologist with HMP YOI Feltham for West London Mental Healthcare Trust.

Dr Eileen Vizard is a consultant child and adolescent psychiatrist for the NSPCC's National Clinical Assessment and Treatment Service (NCATS) and an honorary senior lecturer at UCL.

Contents

	Foreword	**13**
Chapter 1.	**Overview of the Manual**	**15**
	The structure of this book within the manual	16
	Who should use this manual?	16
	How should the intervention described in the manual be delivered?	17
	Is the manual designed to be flexible?	17
	What kind of young person is the manual designed to help?	18
	How do the manual and CD-ROM inter-relate?	19
	What is the character library and how should it be used?	20
	The contents of the accompanying CD-ROM	21
Chapter 2.	**The Treatment Context**	**23**
	Treatment approaches	23
	Cognitive Behavioural Therapy (CBT)	24
	Attachment Theory	26
	Mentalisation Theory	27
	Psychodynamic Psychotherapy	27
	Developmental context	28
	Research context	29
	Early maltreatment and adversity	30
	Poor sexual boundaries	31
	Mental health problems	32
	Psychological and cognitive functioning	32
	Typologies	33
	Emerging personality disorder and psychopathy	33
	'Early onset' and 'late onset' groups	33
	Females who sexually abuse	35
	Treatment of young people with harmful sexual behaviour	36

Chapter 3. Preparing for Intervention — 39
Prior assessment — 39
Measuring risk — 42
Preparing for therapy — 42
Requirements for the clinician — 42
Addressing child protection concerns — 43
Coordination between professionals — 43

Chapter 4. Delivering the Intervention — 47
The aims of intervention — 47
Developing a treatment formulation — 49
Predisposing factors — 49
Attachment and behavioural problems — 49
Beliefs — 52
Precipitating factors — 52
Unmet goals — 52
Strength and protective factors — 52
Overarching goals of treatment — 53
Overarching Goal 1: Building a positive therapeutic alliance — 56
Overarching Goal 2: Building systemic support — 57
The delivery of a typical session — 58
Preparation prior to a session — 58
Delivery of a typical session — 58
Tasks after a session is completed — 60
Working in the room: Ten core treatment components — 61
1. Positive future vision — 61
2. Positive self-narrative — 61
3. Relationships — 62
4. Managing anger — 63
5. Insight: Impact of HSB on self — 64
6. Insight: Impact of HSB on victim — 64
7. Mentalisation ability — 65
8. Understanding and managing HSB — 66
9. Taking responsibility — 67
10. Healthy vs. harmful sexual behaviour — 68
Adapting the manual — 68
Changing the ordering or sequence of sessions — 69
Adapting the manual for adolescents with learning difficulties — 69

Measuring change	72
The Strengths and Difficulties Questionnaire	*72*
Trauma Symptom Checklist for Children	*72*
Rosenberg Self-Esteem Scale	*73*
Adolescent Sexual Behavior Inventory	*73*
Child Behavior Checklist; Youth Self Report	*73*
The NCATS Assessment Questionnaire	*73*
Some thoughts on concurrent work with parents and carers	75

Chapter 5. Module Descriptions — **79**

Module 1: Engagement – Preparing the young person for change — 79
Module 2: Relationships – Cultivating adaptive relationship skills — 85
Module 3: Self-Regulation – 'In the driving seat' — 90
Module 4: Road Map for the Future – Ending and relapse prevention — 97

Appendix I: Sample Session Plans and Home Projects — **101**

Engagement Module Session 1: Making an Authentic Connection — 101
Relationships Module Session 2: Taking Responsibility — 111
Self-Regulation Module Session 6: Detective Work – Clues to My HSB — 125
Road Map for the Future Module Session 4: Staying in the Driving Seat — 134

Appendix II: Sample Material from the Character Library — **149**

References — **153**

Contents of CD-Rom

SESSION PLANS

1. Engagement Module
- Session 1: Making an authentic connection
  - Session plan
  - Home Project: Mapping my future
- Session 2: Looking to the future I
  - Session plan
  - Home Project: Part 1 – Words to describe
  - Home Project: Part 2 – Collage
- Session 3: Looking to the future II
  - Session plan
  - Home Project: Thinking about my skills
- Session 4 (optional): What I believe in
  - Session plan
  - Home Project: Core values for success and happiness

2. Relationships Module
- Session 1: My relationships
  - Session plan
  - Home Project: Friends questionnaire
- Session 2: Taking responsibility
  - Session plan
  - Home Project: Taking responsibility for my achievements
- Session 3: What is sexual abuse?
  - Session plan
  - Home Project: Understanding my own behaviour
- Session 4: Points of view I
  - Session plan
  - Home Project: Points of view
- Session 5: Points of view II
  - Session plan
  - Home Project: Points of view
- Session 6: Understanding my victim's point of view
  - Session plan
  - Home Project: Understanding harmful sexual behaviour: Vignettes
- Session 7: Consequences
  - Session plan
  - Home Project: How my behaviour affected my victim

- Session 8: Boundaries
  - Session plan
  - Home Project: Breaking boundaries: Understanding my own behaviour
- Session 9: Sexual Boundaries
  - Session plan
  - Home Project: New ways to solve old problems

3. Self-Regulation Module
- Session 1: My feelings
  - Session plan
  - Home Project: My feelings
- Session 2: Getting a handle on my feelings
  - Session plan
  - Home Project: Aggression: Pros and Cons
- Session 3: Strategies to deal with harmful sexual thoughts
  - Session plan
  - Home Project: Keeping safe strategies
- Session 4: Dealing with the past and facing the future
  - Session plan
  - Home Project: Moving on from the past
- Session 5: Taking responsibility
  - Session plan
  - Home Project: Part 1 – Credit where credit's due
  - Home Project: Part 2 – Dealing with making mistakes
- Session 6: Detective work: Clues to my HSB
  - Session plan
  - Home Project: Knowing my signals and strategies
- Session 7: Making better choices
  - Session plan
  - Home Project: Making better choices
- Session 8: Anger strategies
  - Session plan
  - Home Project: Part 1 – Anger strategies
  - Home Project: Part 2 – Sex fact sheet

4. Road Map Module
- Session 1: Healthy sexual relationships
  - Session plan
  - Home Project: Understanding my sexual attraction
- Session 2: Sexuality and dating
  - Session plan
  - Home Project: Sexuality fact sheet
- Session 3: Better relationships
  - Session plan
  - Home Project: Relationship skills
- Session 4: Staying in the driving seat
  - Session plan
- Session 5: Ending therapy – Looking towards the future
  - Session plan

CHARACTER LIBRARY

Characters

- ➢ Adults:
  - Female 1
    - Neutral
    - Happy
    - Sad
    - Angry
    - Surprised
    - Puzzled
  - Female 2
    - Neutral
    - Happy
    - Sad
    - Angry
    - Surprised
    - Puzzled
  - Male 1
    - Neutral
    - Happy
    - Sad
    - Angry
    - Surprised
    - Puzzled
  - Male 2
    - Neutral
    - Happy
    - Sad
    - Angry
    - Surprised
    - Puzzled
- ➢ Adolescents
  - Female 1
    - Neutral
    - Happy
    - Sad
    - Angry
    - Surprised
    - Puzzled
  - Female 2
    - Neutral
    - Happy
    - Sad
    - Angry
    - Surprised
    - Puzzled
  - Male 1
    - Neutral
    - Happy
    - Sad
    - Angry
    - Surprised
    - Puzzled
  - Male 2
    - Neutral
    - Happy
    - Sad
    - Angry
    - Surprised
    - Puzzled
- ➢ Latency
  - Female 1
    - Neutral
    - Happy
    - Sad
    - Angry
    - Surprised
    - Puzzled
  - Female 2
    - Neutral
    - Happy
    - Sad
    - Angry
    - Surprised
    - Puzzled
  - Male 1
    - Neutral
    - Happy
    - Sad
    - Angry
    - Surprised
    - Puzzled
  - Male 2
    - Neutral
    - Happy
    - Sad
    - Angry
    - Surprised
    - Puzzled
- ➢ Toddler girl

Locations

- ➢ Bathroom
- ➢ Bedroom
- ➢ Classroom
- ➢ Garden
- ➢ Kitchen
- ➢ Living room
- ➢ Playground
- ➢ Street scene
- ➢ Swimming pool
- ➢ Wood/park

Foreword

The NSPCC is delighted to have supported the development of this therapy manual. Between 20–30 per cent of all sexual offences are committed by young people under the age of 18; to be able to intervene effectively to reduce risk by enabling young people who have exhibited harmful sexual behaviour to lead abuse free and fulfilled lives must be an important child protection and sexual abuse prevention aim.

Over the last decade we have seen real progress in understanding what constitutes an effective assessment of a young person with harmful sexual behaviour. We still need to understand what is most effective in post- assessment interventions and this manual will assist in answering this question. Achieving a balance between respect, hope for and a belief in a positive future as well as enabling a young person to accept responsibility and to understand the motivations and reasons for their behaviour, is a challenging task for social workers, psychologists and other clinicians working with harmful sexual behaviour. This 30 week treatment manual has a foundation in cognitive behavioural therapy and also draws upon attachment, psychodynamic and mentalisation theory and the 'Good Lives' approach which has been influential in informing the development of work with sexual aggression in recent years. It represents a robust and user friendly synthesis of current thinking in work with young people with harmful sexual behaviour and offers practitioners from a range of disciplines an excellent tool and context to enable young people to develop a non abusive and 'coherent sense of self'.

The manual is a significant contribution to the field.

Jon Brown
Head of Strategy and Development
NSPCC

Chapter 1

Overview of the Manual

This manual has been commissioned by the NSPCC to provide a set of therapeutic resources for clinicians working with adolescents in individual treatment who have shown harmful sexual behaviour (HSB). The manual has been designed to be delivered over 30 sessions across four modules, including: Engagement (4 sessions); Relationships (9 sessions); Self-Regulation (8 sessions); Road Map for the Future (5 sessions); and additional clinical work (4 sessions). Each session plan has an associated *home project* for the young person to complete. Electronic versions of session plans and home projects are provided on the CD-ROM included with this book; so readers can see what these look like while reading through the manual, samples of both are also provided at the end of the book.

The four additional sessions scheduled by the clinician should be used primarily to address client-specific issues that the young person may present with and which are not adequately covered in the treatment sessions provided. For example, issues often arise around current difficulties in the young person's home or school life, or relate to unexpected disclosures of prior abuse. These four additional sessions can also be used to cover tasks from the 26 session plans that were not covered because of time constraints.

The goal of the intervention outlined in this manual is to address problematic sexual behaviour within a broader context of the social and emotional challenges faced by adolescents. These are discussed in greater detail in Chapter 4. For now, treatment aims can be summarised as:

1. increasing the likelihood that a young person will show sexual and non-sexual behaviours that are socially acceptable and will refrain from harmful sexual behaviour

2. enhancing the young person's psycho-social functioning, optimism about the future and sense of wellbeing.

The focus of the intervention is strength based – in other words, the aim is to help motivate the young person to engage in a positive process of change, by developing the skills and attitudes required for them to meet the goals that they themselves identify as important at the beginning of treatment. This strength-based work co-occurs with and contributes to change alongside specific interventions to reduce risk of further sexual harm and increase responsibility and the capacity to behave in a sexually appropriate way.

THE STRUCTURE OF THIS BOOK WITHIN THE MANUAL

This book is divided into five main chapters. Chapter 1 provides a brief over view of the nature of the manual, guidance on how it should be used and a summary of the treatment objectives. Chapter 2 provides the relevant background to the work, summarising the theoretical basis for the model, the developmental context (adolescence) and key themes from the research literature. Chapter 3 then presents key considerations relevant to the preparation for any intervention, including the need for an adequate assessment to be conducted prior to treatment. Chapter 4 provides practical advice on delivering the intervention and using the manual in practice; particular emphasis is given to therapeutic strategies that should underpin the clinical approach. Chapter 5 comprises an introduction to each module. At the end of the book we provide an example session plan and home project sheet from each of the four modules. Also included is an illustration of some of the materials available in the character library. Note that all session plans, home project sheets and the full character library are digitally available on the accompanying CD-ROM.

WHO SHOULD USE THIS MANUAL?

This manual has been written for clinicians who are already experienced in clinical work with young people but who may be less familiar in addressing issues of harmful sexual behaviour. Its aim is to provide a comprehensive set of clinical materials to guide individual work with young people across a range of domains – not just sexual behaviour. All experienced clinicians, irrespective of background, should be able to access and make use of this material, but we do assume an existing knowledge of therapeutic experience with at-risk adolescents, their families, carers and allied professionals. It is important to highlight from the outset that this manual does not represent a 'one size fits all' approach that should be delivered in an identical fashion to all young people. Rather it should be seen as a *clinical resource* that should be delivered in a thoughtful and flexible way depending on the needs of the particular adolescent in therapy.

HOW SHOULD THE INTERVENTION DESCRIBED IN THE MANUAL BE DELIVERED?

It is fair to say that most adolescents presenting with HSB elicit high levels of anxiety in professional networks partly because of the serious risks associated with their behaviour. Behaviours that entail sexual harm, even when they are of low frequency, can have serious criminal and placement implications and a profound impact on schooling and peer relationships for adolescents, not to mention traumatic and enduring effects experienced by the victims of any abuse. Therefore we do not recommend that this kind of intervention is conducted by a lone professional. While the therapy itself may be delivered by either one or two clinicians in the room (the latter is often preferable, with one clinician of either gender if resources permit) *it should always be delivered in an inter-agency and interdisciplinary context*. This will not only stabilise the individual therapy but provide a context for systemic change and a framework to monitor and address ongoing risk. Given the often challenging nature of the material and the child protection risks which are inherent in the work, regular and experienced supervision is essential for all clinicians, irrespective of their own level of experience. It can also be helpful for managers to ensure that clinical teams have a space where they are able to address the conflicts, anxieties and dynamics that can be associated with this work. There may, for example, be conflicts in the broader professional network that stem from divergent views of the young person as victim or callous perpetrator that need to be managed alongside the demands of the individual therapy work. Here, colleagues co-working the case but not actually co-delivering the treatment in the room are often better placed to manage these dynamics. In a similar way, an incident of harmful sexual behaviour during therapy is likely to be stressful for the treating clinician, who will require advice and support from colleagues to ensure an adequate inter-agency response. A well functioning team should be able to address these problems both on a practical level (e.g. by facilitating communication among professionals and implementing effective child protection safe-guards) but also at a clinical level (e.g. by reflecting on how the work is impacting on interpersonal team dynamics). Trust, honesty and a commitment to collaboration between colleagues, and adequate supervision within a well managed team, will provide a stable foundation for the delivery of the individual therapeutic intervention.

IS THE MANUAL DESIGNED TO BE FLEXIBLE?

The manual is structured with sessions and modules presented in a particular order. Inevitably there will sometimes be tension between clinician flexibility, the need to individualise the treatment for a given young person and adherence to the guidance provided. In other words, it may be helpful and indeed necessary to alter this structure depending on the presenting problems of the adolescent to be treated. The *Change for Good* approach in this treatment manual is designed to provide an experienced clinician with a range of materials to address HSB in a wide variety of adolescents. It cannot cover every eventuality, nor can it be written in a way that would meet the needs of each individual young person. We would therefore encourage clinicians to use this manual in a creative way by tailoring it to the needs of each adolescent. We recognise that individual events, crises related to the young person's behaviour or family and problems with engagement may all require a clinician to reflect on how best to adapt the programme as presented here. For example, it may be necessary to defer a planned skill training element until the next session, or spend a much greater part of a session addressing a current problem. Such changes should be balanced with the need to cover the material that will help the adolescent manage their emotional and behavioural problems more effectively in the longer term. In other words, clinicians should remain mindful of how their choices impact on meeting overall treatment aims.

In addition we would like to highlight that a flexible approach is desirable. The manual has been written in a way such that the content of each session is often rather full; indeed, sometimes not all tasks in a session may be covered. The choice of tasks has been presented to give the clinician maximum flexibility – not to constrain them with a weekly challenge to cover every item. What is important is that the clinician aims to achieve the primary goal for each session by adapting the session plan, taking into account the needs of the young person and their current concerns. In other words, *the manual should inform not replace clinical judgement*. One way to manage the material to be covered is to regard the overall programme as a 30-session intervention, thus allowing four 'free' sessions that can be used to address salient individual issues for the particular adolescent in therapy. Space within the programme for such individualised work may even be regarded as essential to the success of treatment.

WHAT KIND OF YOUNG PERSON IS THE MANUAL DESIGNED TO HELP?

The manual has been primarily aimed at addressing HSB in male adolescents without learning disability. Given that this group represents the majority of any community referrals it was decided at the outset that the manual in this format would have the widest impact and relevance. In Chapter 4 we provide some guidance as to how the manual may be adapted to work with individuals with learning difficulties and some discussion of HSB in females is provided in Chapter 2. The manual will not be equally relevant to all cases and it is highly likely that many young people in treatment will have additional therapeutic needs beyond the scope of this programme that will require intervention (e.g. depression; PTSD; anxiety caused by placement change). In other words, while the manual may provide some core therapeutic materials, each clinician should ensure that a comprehensive intervention is provided. As suggested above, this material may be presented in four supplementary sessions to create a 30-session programme.

HOW DO THE MANUAL AND CD-ROM INTER-RELATE?

The resources for this manual are provided in two parts. The first is this printed book, which provides background and practical guidance on how the intervention should be delivered. Note that comprehensive guidance on how to conduct an assessment of HSB is not provided. It is assumed that adolescents, prior to beginning this intervention, have already been assessed. Topics covered in this book include:

- setting the treatment context for intervention
- key themes from the research literature
- a description of core treatment areas
- guidance on structuring a session
- working with carers
- modifying the intervention for adolescents with learning disability.

The second part of this resource is the accompanying CD-ROM which includes electronic versions of each of the 26 individual session plans and home projects. These are provided in an electronic format so that they can be easily printed out and used by the clinician in a flexible way. The CD-ROM also contains the 'character library' that is described in more detail below as well as sex and sexuality information sheets.

The sessions are divided into four modules described in Chapter 5 of this book and included in full detail in the CD-ROM.

Engagement module (4 sessions)

The sessions within this module aim to establish a good rapport and therapeutic alliance with the young person, and provide a focus to promote their motivation to change.

Relationships module (9 sessions)

This module is focused on developing the young person's general relationship skills and in particular perspective taking. Later sessions address their harmful sexual behaviour and their relationship with their victim.

Self-Regulation module (8 sessions)

These sessions focus on the young person's internal world – their thoughts, feelings and beliefs – and aim to develop the capacity to regulate emotions (particularly anger and sexual arousal) more adaptively.

Road Map for the Future module (5 sessions)

This final module deals with issues of sexuality, dating, ending and relapse prevention.

Additional sessions (4 sessions)

Four additional sessions should be scheduled to provide time for work not completed in the 26 formalised sessions. These sessions are also essential to provide scope for addressing individual issues brought by the young person in treatment.

The total programme should be delivered across 30 sessions. One sample session from each module is provided at the end of this book. All other session plans are stored electronically in the CD-ROM provided.

WHAT IS THE CHARACTER LIBRARY AND HOW SHOULD IT BE USED?

One innovative aspect of this manual is the development of a specially commissioned library of characters and settings that can be used in-session to help the young person explore real and fictional scenarios. These characters span a broad range of ages, from toddler to adult. Each character is provided in six formats that reflect six different facial expressions (neutral, angry, surprised, happy, sad and puzzled). Examples of these characters are shown at the end of this book along with examples of the range of facial expressions provided. In addition the library also comprises ten 'background scenes' including: a living room, bedroom, kitchen, bathroom, garden, street, swimming pool, park, playground and classroom. These are common settings for normative adolescent behaviours and they have also been chosen as the most frequent places where adolescents displaying HSB target their victims.

While the characters in the library are used to illustrate several session or home project tasks *their primary function is to serve as a creative resource for the clinician and young person in the room.* It is recommended that prior to beginning a new treatment case each figure is printed, cut out and laminated and several A3 versions of the background settings are printed. This will provide the clinician with a 'tool box' that can be drawn on in many different ways. For example, when discussing with an adolescent a fictional vignette, the clinician may decide to illustrate the events using the character library. The adolescent can choose the figures that best represent the characters and arrange the scene on the appropriate background. Such an approach can help shift the focus of both the young person and the clinician onto a neutral space and can help in actively engaging them with the material, particularly useful for those young people for whom engagement is an issue. Other examples of how the character library can be helpful include the following:

- The pictorial vignette can be used as a forum to explore what each character is thinking and feeling and develop perspective taking (sometimes using thought bubbles).

- A figure may be selected with one emotional expression, but the clinician may ask the young person to identify the facial expression of what the character is *really* feeling inside.

- How close the figures are together can be used to gauge and vary appropriate personal space.

- Relative sizes of the figures (e.g. the teenager and latency males) can be used to reflect and consider power imbalances that may otherwise be minimised.

- Different stages of a scenario can be constructed in order to highlight particular 'choice points' in that scenario.

- The figures may be used to represent real people in the young person's life in order to recreate actual experiences that may be difficult to describe in a verbal fashion.

The character library should therefore be seen as a resource to be drawn on and used throughout the therapy to improve engagement, provide a reference point to challenge distorted thinking and, most important, to provide a vehicle to develop mentalisation capacities.

THE CONTENTS OF THE ACCOMPANYING CD-ROM

The accompanying CD-ROM contains 26 detailed session plans across all four modules and their associated home project sheets. It also includes the character library that can be used as a resource for many of the therapeutic tasks.

Chapter 2

The Treatment Context

TREATMENT APPROACHES

Our treatment approach has been informed by a number of theoretical models. In the absence of convincing evidence that any particular treatment model is more clinically effective we have drawn on evidence-based and clinically established approaches and integrated them in a framework in which the adolescent's thoughts, feelings and behaviours are addressed, alongside their sense of self and the nature of their relationships to others. Below we highlight key aspects of each of the models relevant to this programme, which are:

- cognitive behavioural therapy
- attachment theory
- psychodynamic psychotherapy
- mentalisation
- systems theory.

We have drawn these models together in a way that builds a strength based and constructive approach without losing sight of the negative and inherently harmful nature of HSB. One excellent example in the field in relation to treatment for sexual offenders is Ward and colleagues' 'Good Lives' model (GLM) (Thakker, Ward and Tidmarsh, 2006). The GLM places the traditional risk-need approach in a broader framework such that the aim of intervention is to broaden interpersonal functioning in order to help people find ways of meeting their needs more adaptively and appropriately. At its heart, the GLM contends that, by focusing too much on future offending, there is a failure to promote more positive and constructive behaviours, attitudes and skills that are the very elements which can *offset* risk. Many juvenile HSB interventions (derived from adult sex offender models) typify this stance with treatment goals focusing on harmful sexual behaviour (i.e. on young people accepting/understanding their behaviour and the 'offence cycle'). There is often an emphasis on *reducing* unhealthy sexual thoughts, *avoiding* people, places and activities viewed as 'high-risk' and *eliminating* inappropriate or harmful behaviours. By contrast, our manual with its ethos *Change for Good*, expressed in the subtitle, like the GLM sees risk being reduced by helping individuals develop socially acceptable ways to attain their goals; in other words finding alternative appropriate ways to meet needs that were previously attained by inappropriate (and criminogenic) behaviours. As a result, this approach places greater emphasis on treating underlying causes rather than simply the undesired (sexually abusive) behaviours.

To succeed with this approach it is necessary to have a therapeutic agenda which addresses those factors that underpin a 'good life', both internal (skills and abilities) and external (stable support systems). The *Change for Good* approach aims to develop both the adolescent's positive goals for the future by enhancing their interpersonal relationship skills alongside their ability to regulate and understand their emotional experience. This arguably has a number of incidental advantages in addition to creating more adaptive ways for an adolescent to meet their legitimate goals compared to a more traditional focus on negative behaviours, vigilance and avoidance. First, it creates a more positive therapeutic context, which is likely to facilitate a sound therapeutic alliance, a key factor in treatment outcome for children and adolescents (Eltz, Shirk and Sarlin, 1995). Second, the central role played by identity formation in adolescence sits comfortably with an intervention aimed at promoting a positive sense of current and future self.

Although the work described in this manual relates to individual work with a young person it cannot be emphasised enough that this form of intervention needs to be embedded in a systemic context. Guidance from the Department of Health provides the framework within which professionals should work and this should be familiar reading to all clinicians planning to deliver this kind of intervention. The guidance *Working Together to Safeguard Children* was recently updated in March 2010 and is available to download from the Department of Children, Schools and Families website (DCSF, 2010). This guidance stems from a systemic model in which the young person is seen as one aspect of a dynamic and extended system, including the family, community, schools, and all professionals and organisations involved in the care of the child. In addition to this statutory guidance the clinician should be familiar to some degree with systemic models of working in a clinical context. (See the paper by Bentovim, 2004 for an excellent overview describing an integrated systems approach to working with families in the context of abuse.)

Cognitive Behavioural Therapy (CBT)

The primary treatment model that underpins the work outlined in this manual is cognitive behavioural in nature. CBT interventions have gained widespread popularity and empirical support for a range of emotional and behavioural problems in children and adults and they are founded on the central tenet that thoughts, beliefs and cognitive strategies alongside environmental contingencies shape how we behave (Beck, 1979; Beck, 1995). Emotional and behavioural problems are treated by helping clients identify, test out and change underlying beliefs, assumptions and thoughts they hold about the world, themselves and the future. This is achieved in a context of an explicit exploration of the relationship between their thoughts and feelings.

CBT in the context of the juvenile treatment of HSB has often veered towards a rather standardised psycho-educational approach where exercises relate to 'thinking errors' and 'cognitive distortions' with little genuine exploration of an adolescent's underlying beliefs and schemas about the world. This is consistent with a general tendency in CBT approaches for child conduct problems; these have typically aimed to improve social skills, problem solving ability, and anger management (McCrory and Farmer, 2009). There has been much less emphasis on changing latent mental structures which contain meanings about the self and others – schemas or core beliefs which organise and guide how an individual perceives themselves and interprets the world around them; these can also be thought about as internal working models or scripts. While a focus on identifying and restructuring such schemas play a core part in the treatment of affective disorders such as depression and anxiety they have been much less prominent in the treatment of conduct disorder in general, and HSB in particular.

Children who behave in a way that harms others sexually typically hold more negative and aggressive views of themselves and others. Of course, for a minority, these are skewed in the other direction, and are unrealistically positive. Challenging underlying assumptions, encouraging adolescents to expand the 'evidence' they use to inform their beliefs, and making shifts in how evidence is evaluated (and not dismissed) all serve to create an alternative (more balanced) set of core beliefs in an ongoing process of cognitive restructuring. It is important to acknowledge that what therapy might in fact be achieving is the development of a set of more adaptive schemas about the world rather than the reconfiguration of old ones. In this manual, with its *Change for Good* approach, strategies that target latent meaning structures, such as continuum work and narrative techniques, are placed alongside strategies that are geared explicitly to change behavioural patterns and challenge distorted thinking.

In addition, it is worth highlighting collaboration as a key feature of the CBT model and one which has also often been downplayed in work with children and adolescents. Collaboration means that both the client and clinician work together to understand the presenting difficulties and create a shared view of the problem(s). While the clinician brings specialist skills and knowledge the client is an expert in their own experience and will bring their own set of strengths and resources. The advantage of creating an active collaboration between the client and the clinician is that it increases the likelihood that the client will attribute improvement in their problems to their own efforts. Such an approach is quite different from how CBT, certainly in child forensic populations, is often delivered. Adopting a 'psycho-educational' stance risks making the adolescent feel that therapy is something that is being imposed on them rather than something that they are an active and joint participant in. We would encourage clinicians using this manual actively to engage adolescents and genuinely to consider their views and suggestions; for example, in relation to issues they wish to discuss which they are invited to raise at the beginning of each session. We have structured the sessions so that there is a space for such discussion and although some tasks may at times need to be cut short to accommodate it the benefits in the longer term are likely to be significant. Of course, such a collaborative stance needs to co-exist with maintaining boundaries and not colluding with an adolescent's distorted thinking. There is a difference between collaboration and the adolescent having free rein to determine the nature of the therapy. This is the collaborative balance that needs to be achieved and although we may not get it right in every session it is better to try than rigidly to adhere to a preordained protocol that is likely ultimately to alienate the young person in treatment.

The idea of seeking to work on a collaborative basis with clients who may be ambivalent or indeed hostile may seem quite surprising to some forensic clinicians. In our view listening to and acknowledging an adolescent's viewpoint, and acting on it if appropriate (even if it is in a small way), can help make them feel that they are an individual with valuable and valid opinions that can shape how things are done. It is arguable that this feeling of empowerment can help increase their sense of self-efficacy that will also apply to their own efforts at personal change; it also is a concrete way in which the adolescent is made to feel that they are a participant rather than the subject in their own therapy. In the room, this can at times feel uncomfortable for the clinician who may think they are allowing a diversion from the main journey of the programme. But in practice going along with these 'excursions' can be a powerful tool in cementing the alliance and creating a forum for important material to emerge.

Attachment Theory

There has been an increasing interest in the role of attachment in relation to sexual offending (see Rich, 2006 for an excellent and comprehensive overview). In line with the original model put forward by Bowlby (1969), we understand a normative attachment framework during development as a key factor that underpins adaptive and autonomous personality functioning. Many of the maltreatment experiences of young people presenting with harmful sexual behaviour are at the hands of caregivers, typically parents, step parents and older siblings. Unsurprisingly many show attachment problems; over half of children and young people referred to our treatment service were found to show features of insecure attachment (e.g. over-familiarity with strangers; failure to seek comfort from caregivers when distressed; responding in a contradictory manner to caregivers). This is hardly surprising when one considers that, alongside their experiences of abuse, there is typically a high level of placement instability (35% had six or more placement moves by the time they were assessed in early adolescence), marital breakdown (73%) and placement in care (76%) (Hickey *et al.*, 2006). The internal working models constructed by these young people are likely to be characterised by features of instability, threat and vulnerability which will have served to undermine their development of a sense of agency and capacity for mentalisation – the ability to reflect on their own and others' thoughts, feelings and intentions.

Mentalisation Theory

Mentalisation combines elements of psychoanalytic, attachment and social cognitive theory and represents a relatively new approach to psychological intervention for a range of disorders (Fonagy *et al.*, 2002). It partly stems from the philosophical and empirical work on 'theory of mind' – a uniquely human ability that allows us to make sense of our own actions and those of others by representing intentional mental states such as desires, beliefs and feelings. Failing to adequately represent such states in oneself and others can contribute to different forms of psychopathology, both at the individual and systemic levels. Mentalisation, while being a shared process, can give rise to marked individual differences in the beliefs we hold, as each of us is influenced by our own attention to aspects of the environment and our internal implicit and explicit (autobiographical) memory. These individual differences are in part influenced by early attachment experience which informs how our internal working models or schemata develop; these in turn shape our sense of self and how we relate to others. The capacity to mentalise adaptively is hypothesized to depend on an adequate attachment experience which provides the scaffolding required to develop an adequate meta-cognitive system to represent mental states and emotions.

Within the psychotherapeutic context, mentalisation-focused intervention operates to promote four aspects of mentalising ability, in relation to:

- other people's thoughts and feelings (for example, being able to take the perspective of someone else)
- one's own mental life (for example, being curious and aware of one's own thoughts with the capacity to consider how emotions – or in the case of HSB, sexual arousal – may distort understanding)
- self-representation (for example, having a rich and coherent autobiographical narrative)
- values and attitudes (for example, cognitive styles that allow for non-black and white thinking and flexibility – an openness to change in response to feedback).

As discussed later, many children who present with harmful sexual behaviour have experienced one or more forms of maltreatment. The same environments which set the scene for such environmental adversity are almost always accompanied by an increased likelihood of impaired attachment experiences (Rich, 2006).

Psychodynamic Psychotherapy

There is a relatively established consensus that psychodynamic approaches are less effective compared to other approaches (notably systemic interventions) in treating conduct problems in children (Fonagy *et al.*, 2005). Nevertheless, many of the constructs and techniques associated with these approaches can play a valuable role in making sense of adolescents with complex presentations. In the context of the *Change for Good* approach we would highlight the importance accorded to the therapeutic relationship. The collaborative relationship enshrined in CBT can be complemented by a psychodynamic model, which seeks to understand how the client-therapist relationship can serve to influence the nature and progress of therapy. Transference and counter-transference are useful constructs in conceptualising the conflictual feelings that a clinician can experience working with a young person who is at varying times aggressive, compliant, vulnerable and callous. Such feelings can often be understood in a treatment formulation where past influences and relationships are considered as influential factors in how a young person currently conceptualises and interacts with the world (which can also be thought about in terms of an internal working model).

For example, the clinician may at times represent for the young person their 'abuser', the therapeutic context recreating a past adult relationship where they were made to feel powerless and demeaned. This can elicit reactions that are well beyond the actual therapeutic relationship but represent prior experiences of victimisation by the young person. Such reactions may include hostile behaviours but equally they may arise in the form of sexualised behaviour towards the clinician who unconsciously they are seeking to please. This sexualised approach is likely to be consistent with the adolescent's prior experience of being groomed by their abuser who may have rewarded and normalised such behaviours. When both a male and female clinician are co-working the case in the room, differential responses to either gender can be highly informative about how the young person has internalised relationships in a sexual way; in some cases this arises in the form of rather chauvinistic attitudes to a female clinician who is ignored in favour of the male clinician who is given attention and respect. Thinking about these relational aspects of the therapeutic relationship in a psychodynamic frame can help make sense of what can often appear to be contradictory and erratic behaviours in the young person.

DEVELOPMENTAL CONTEXT

This manual has been developed in order to assist with individual therapeutic work with adolescents showing harmful sexual behaviour. While we focus primarily on these behavioural problems, it is important to bear in mind the particular developmental challenges that arise in adolescence. This is a period characterised by a set of changes that occur in physical, cognitive, emotional and social domains. Physically, changes are driven by increased levels of gonadal hormones (notably testosterone in boys and estradiol in girls). The magnitude and speed of these (and other) hormonal changes are unparalleled compared to other stages of development. These changes lead to an increase in growth, sexual maturation, and secondary sex characteristics. They also lead to a cascade of brain changes, in both structure and function. As children change physically, and become more adult-like, they also begin to be treated by the world differently.

The complex set of changes in adolescence is hypothesised to be related to those factors that lead to a window of vulnerability characterised by increased risk taking, sensation seeking and heightened emotions. Much of the brain development which occurs at this time is related to those brain areas that play a key role in regulating behaviour and emotion, and perceiving and evaluating risk and reward (the most important of these is the prefrontal cortex). One influential view is that a period of vulnerability arises from the disjunction between behavioural and cognitive systems in the developing brain: early in puberty, there is an increase in emotional arousability and sensation seeking, but it is only by late adolescence that the maturation of frontal brain systems provides a framework for adequate regulatory competence (Steinberg, 2005). However, this period of vulnerability is also a period of plasticity and opportunity that can be used to help scaffold and foster regulatory competence. At an individual level such competence is reflected in a more sophisticated mentalisation ability, while at the social level it can reflect a shift from family to extended pro-social networks. Peer relationships in particular take on a new and influential role, as does the adolescent's sense of self.

At a psycho-social level Erikson's theory of identity formation in adolescence, the fifth of eight stages in his theory of developmental progression from birth to old age, centres on the need to forge a coherent sense of self (Erikson, 1959–1980). This process of identity formation is necessary to move towards an adult stage where the individual has the capacity for intimacy, love and work. Sexual activity may play a role in identity conflict. Erikson believed that, during early adolescence, there can be constructive experimentation with roles; in our view, with adolescents presenting with HSB, there is a risk that a 'negative identity' characterised by sexual behaviour can predominate in the absence of opportunities to develop a positive, more adaptive self-conceptualisation. One goal in this manual is to help the young person create a positive sense of who they are despite their past harmful behaviours, and at the same time construct a way to view their own sexuality, and sexual behaviour in general, in a way that is positive and acceptable. Understood in this context it is clear that these young people and their HSB differ significantly from adults who sexually offend (Hackett, Masson and Phillips, 2006). In later adolescence, a clear sexual identity is established as the adolescent identifies role models to inspire them and develops a set of ideals to live by. In this manual a positive elaborated vision of the future using a visual timeline provides a forum for the young person to envision and experiment with how they would like to see their future selves develop.

RESEARCH CONTEXT

There is now a well-established evidence base in relation to harmful sexual behaviour in young people (see Barbaree and Marshall, 2005 and Rich, 2003 for excellent reviews of the field). While we know that adolescents constitute around 20 per cent of all sexual offenders (Home Office, 2003) the nature of sexual offending is such that this figure is likely to be a marked under-estimate of the actual prevalence. Such behaviours are often undisclosed or kept secret and as a result fail to elicit appropriate professional intervention or criminal proceedings.

In this section we provide a selective overview of several key themes that characterise the research literature on HSB in children and adolescents. Some familiarity with these themes and the evidence base in general is important for any clinician about to embark on an individual programme of therapy. Two key points frame the research in this area. First is the fact that children and adolescents displaying HSB are a highly heterogeneous group. So while the research literature can help us generate clinical hypotheses we must take care not to jump to conclusions nor to make inappropriate generalisations in individual cases. A second point that emerges is that not all adolescents with HSB go on to become sexual offenders as adults; the evidence suggests that only a minority do so, with many more proceeding to become engaged in *other* forms of illegal behaviours (Worling and Curwen, 2000). This observation highlights the relationship between HSB and conduct problems in general and has a number of implications regarding treatment. We would suggest that while harmful sexual behaviours have certain unique features (mainly in relation to disturbed sexual development and dysregulation of sexual responses) they share many common features with general delinquent behaviours. In one study, for example, we found that half of all young people with HSB referred to our service met diagnostic criteria for conduct disorder, and that over 90 per cent had experienced one form of maltreatment – a common risk factor for general delinquency (Vizard *et al.*, 2007a). Consequently this *Change for Good* manual has been constructed as a holistic treatment model in which problematic sexual behaviours are addressed in the wider context of poor emotional and behavioural regulation.

Early maltreatment and adversity

Typically a matrix of adverse developmental experiences precedes the onset of HSB in children including sexual, physical and emotional abuse, neglect and domestic violence (Righthand and Welch, 2004; Vizard *et al.*, 2007a). It is important to note that these experiences are general developmental risk factors for a wide array of psychological disorders, as well as for anti-social behaviour. While the experience of sexual abuse in particular is more frequent in children with HSB compared to the general population the evidence is mixed when the comparison is made between adolescent sexual and non-sexual offenders (van Wijk *et al.*, 2006). For example, Burton, Miller and Shill (2002) in a study of over 300 adolescents found that 79.4 per cent of sexual offenders had reported being sexually victimised compared to 46.7 per cent of non-sexual offenders. In other words the experience of sexual abuse does not uniquely characterise children with HSB compared to those with general delinquency problems; equally, sexual victimisation is not experienced by all children showing HSB.

Burton reported a number of abuse factors that were significantly associated with those who proceeded to sexually offend, including: having been abused by both males and females; being physically coerced; and having experienced penetrative abuse (Burton *et al.*, 2002). In a prospective longitudinal study of children who had been sexually abused Salter and colleagues found that only 12 per cent had recorded incidents of sexually abusing later in life. This study highlighted several factors distinct from the abuse itself (notably material neglect; lack of supervision; interfamilial violence) that were associated with later sexually abusive behaviour (Salter *et al.*, 2003).

The emerging consensus, therefore, is that with delinquency in general some early adversity in the form of abuse or neglectful parenting (not always severe) characterises many of the children who display HSB (Righthand and Welch, 2004). In a recent UK sample a higher prevalence of parental mental health problems, parental criminality and relationship breakdown was reported (Vizard *et al.*, 2007a). This 'matrix of adversity' is likely to be complex and reflect the interaction of a range of factors including a child's age, coping ability, parental relationships and support network, the duration and form of the abuse, the relationship to the abuser and the circumstances around disclosure. At one level it is possible to view HSB as a behavioural marker reflecting a significant disturbance in normative self-regulation following an abusive developmental experience.

Poor sexual boundaries

As noted above, children and adolescents who present with HSB may have been exposed to lax sexual boundaries in the home. In one study, 50 per cent had witnessed sexual behaviour among adults or had access to sexually explicit material (Vizard *et al.*, 2007a); other studies have highlighted the exposure to pornography at a young age (Wieckowski *et al.*, 1998). Therefore, in the absence of a history of sexual abuse, it is important to establish during any assessment whether a child presenting with HSB has been inappropriately exposed to sexual material or behaviour.

The impact of the increased accessibility of internet pornography in families where there is poor parental supervision is unknown. At the time of writing there is a recognition among researchers and clinicians that internet use as well as the role of other digital technology in HSB (for example, use of mobile phones) is a priority area for future research. Our clinical experience is that digital pornography is increasingly a common feature of cases referred for assessment and its role has manifested in a number of specific ways. For example, the digital medium may:

- *constitute part of the abuse:* for example an adolescent may show a victim pornographic images as part of the grooming process, or an offender may use webcam technology to actively abuse children over the internet

- *reinforce sexual deviance:* by providing a forum to elaborate deviant sexual fantasies, for example about younger children or siblings

- *facilitate extreme and premature sexual preoccupation:* by providing unlimited and developmentally inappropriate access to pornography in the context of lax parental supervision.

Mental health problems

A number of studies have reported mental health problems and disorders in a subset of the population of young people displaying HSB. Conduct Disorder (CD) is particularly common, and has been reported to be the most common DSM diagnosis in this group (Kavoussi, Kaplan and Becker, 1988: 48%; Vizard *et al.*, 2007a: 50%). It should be noted, however, that the HSB itself is likely to contribute significantly to meeting the diagnostic criteria for CD. As with non-sexually offending delinquents, adolescents with HSB with an early onset of conduct problems are more likely to show non-sexual offending (Butler and Seto, 2002).

Post-Traumatic Stress Disorder (PTSD) and Reactive Attachment Disorder have also been reported as well as attentional and impulse control problems in the form of Attention-Deficit Hyperactivity Disorder (ADHD) (Kavoussi *et al.*, 1988; Vizard *et al.* 2007a). These disorders, however, are present in only a minority and are therefore not likely to represent a sufficient causal explanation for the emergence of sexual behaviour problems. In some instances, notably in relation to PTSD, they may contribute directly to HSB. For example, McMackin and colleagues (2002) in a study of 40 male sex offenders between the ages of 12 and 17 years reported that traumatic experiences and related emotions may have acted as triggers for HSB. Given the prevalence of physical, sexual and emotional abuse in this population, alongside the potentially traumatic experiences of acting as an abuser, it will be necessary for any effective intervention to address PTSD symptomatology.

Psychological and cognitive functioning

While a significant proportion of young people with HSB may have learning difficulties, it is not the case that such behaviour is more prevalent in young people with learning difficulties overall (Hackett, Masson and Phillips, 2003; O'Callaghan, 1998). However, learning difficulties appear to be more common in young people with HSB in the same way that they are more common in young people with general conduct problems.

In two studies reporting the characteristics of young people referred to two UK HSB services some degree of learning disability was reported to characterise between a quarter and half (O'Callaghan, 1998; Vizard *et al.*, 2007a). At the same time it should be noted that a significant proportion of young people referred to such services will have no intellectual difficulties at all (Taylor, 2003). Accurate evaluation of the distribution and nature of learning difficulties in this population remains an outstanding task for future research.

Learning difficulties are unlikely to represent a causal explanation for a young person's HSB, but again they may represent an important factor in any treatment formulation. Assessing a young person's IQ can be important to establish their capacity to understand and process information in the home, at school or in therapy. Sometimes, for example, inappropriate expectations of an adolescent's intellectual ability mean that their behaviour is inappropriately interpreted as wilful defiance rather than simply a failure to adequately understand or retain information or requests. Any intervention will need to take account of social and cognitive functioning including how shorter attention spans may impact on the therapeutic process (Hackett *et al.*, 2003). Although this manual with its *Change for Good* approach has not been specifically designed for adolescents with learning difficulties, many of its components are suitable for this group and can be amended to take into account lower levels of cognitive functioning (see Chapter 4).

Typologies

There have been a number of attempts to rationalise the heterogeneity in this group of young people by developing classifications based on causal factors or motivation (e.g. experimentation versus sexual aggression), the nature of the HSB (e.g. rape), or the victims targeted (children versus peers) (O'Brien and Bera, 1986; Prentky *et al.*, 2000). As an illustration, Prentky and colleagues in their paper of actuarial risk assessment (Prentky *et al.*, 2000) rationally derived the following categories from their sample of 96 juvenile sexual offenders who ranged from 9 to 20 years of age: Child Molester (69%); Rapists (12.5%); Sexually Reactive Children (6.25%); Paraphilic Offender (3%); Fondler (3%); and Unclassifiable (6.25%). Developing such categories within a research context may, over time, help inform risk assessment approaches at the clinical level. However, at the current time such typologies are not sufficiently robust adequately to capture the complexity and heterogeneity in the presentation of young people in HSB (Rich, 2003, p.96); much more evidence is required to establish categories with face and predictive validity.

Emerging personality disorder and psychopathy

More recently attention has focused on the role of personality traits and empathic functioning in children displaying Emerging Severe Personality Disorder (ESPD) traits (Vizard *et al.*, 2007b). This subgroup is defined as scoring more highly on a childhood measure of psychopathy (Psychopathy Checklist – Youth Version (PCL-YV; Forth, Kosson and Hare, 2003) and on measures of conduct problems; these children tend in particular to have empathy deficits reflected in elevated callous-unemotional traits. While they are not characterised by a greater incidence of maltreatment, these young people are more likely to have: parents with mental health problems; an early difficult temperament and aggression; behavioural problems at school; and a history of cruelty to animals. It is notable that their harmful sexual behaviour is more predatory in nature in that they are more likely to groom victims, target a range of victims, and use verbal and physical coercion (Vizard *et al.*, 2007b). This subgroup may represent a minority of individuals with HSB who may be at higher risk of later violent offending (Vizard *et al.*, 2007b).

'Early onset' and 'late onset' groups

The HSB population has also been studied by contrasting those young people whose sexual behaviour problems emerged in pre-adolescence versus those for whom such behaviours emerged for the first time during adolescence. These groups have been characterised as 'early onset' and 'late onset' groups. McCrory and colleagues (McCrory et al., 2008) explored whether young people with an early onset of sexually harmful behaviour conform to a developmental taxonomy originally conceptualised for generic anti-social behaviour (Moffitt, 1993). Moffitt suggested that a small group of children pursue a life-course persistent path of anti-social behaviour from preschool to adulthood (Moffitt, 1993, 2006). She specifically proposed that early deficits in cognitive functioning, self-regulation and temperament are manifest at the behavioural level early in these children and that these factors heighten a child's vulnerability to criminogenic influences and social adversity including parental mental health problems, harsh and inconsistent discipline, and changes in primary caretaker (Moffitt and Caspi, 2001). By adulthood it was proposed that these individuals are likely to present with higher levels of violent aggression, psychopathic personality traits, and mental health problems (Moffitt, 2006). Yet during adolescence the behavioural manifestations of those with an early onset of anti-social behaviour are superficially similar to those whose anti-social behaviour begins first in adolescence, even though for the latter the underlying reasons for the behaviours are thought to be quite different (a motivation to achieve adult status and peer acceptance; Moffitt, 1993).

McCrory and colleagues (2008) compared children with an early and late onset of HSB and found that individuals in the early onset group were more likely to have experienced maltreatment from an early age (much more commonly before the age of 6 years) compared to those who began their HSB in adolescence. The early onset group also presented with more signs of neuropsychological risk in terms of poor temperament, hyperactivity, and poorer intellectual functioning. These young people also had higher scores on a psychopathy measure and greater mental health intervention consistent with a greater likelihood of higher levels of callousness and mental health problems respectively later in life. During the adolescent period the sexual and non-sexual behavioural presentations of those on both early and late onset trajectories were found to be similar. Notably, however, the victims they targeted differed: those in the early onset group were less discriminating and more likely to abuse males and females. With regard to non-sexual anti-social behaviour (physical aggression, stealing, and cruelty to animals), fewer differences were found during the adolescent period, while in the pre-adolescent period the early onset group displayed higher levels of each of these behaviours, highlighting a developmental continuity in deficient behavioural regulation for these young people.

These findings suggest that children with a pre-adolescent onset of HSB are likely to have had more severe experiences of environmental adversity combined with higher levels of neuropsychological and temperamental vulnerability. It is thought that the interaction between these factors place these young people at greater risk of a lifelong pattern of maladjustment and anti-social presentation (McCrory et al., 2008; Moffitt, 1993, 2006). As such, it is crucial to consider the developmental history of any adolescent presenting for treatment in relation to prior maltreatment, continuity of conduct problems and the timing of their first episode of harmful sexual behaviour and whether this was prior to (younger than 11 years) or during adolescence (older than 11 years of age).

Females who sexually abuse

As noted by Hickey and colleagues (Hickey *et al.*, 2008) cultural attitudes towards female sexuality do not sit easily with the phenomenon of female perpetrated sexual aggression, whether in juveniles or adults (Hetherton, 1999). Nevertheless, official estimates suggest that female juveniles account for approximately 9 per cent of arrests for sexual offences and 2 per cent of forcible rapes (Snyder, 2005). The dearth of research on female juveniles may be due in part to the fact that relatively few such individuals come to the attention of assessment and treatment services. This contributes to a major methodological limitation when investigating gender effects: namely, small sample sizes. Consequently we are only able to draw tentative conclusions about the similarities and differences between the genders.

In one of the larger studies Mathews, Hunter and Vuz (1997) compared 67 female (aged 11 to 18 years) and 70 male (aged 11 to 17 years) juveniles who sexually abused. However, because the data for the two samples was collected using different methodologies, between-group statistical comparisons were not possible. A greater proportion of females (77.6%) than males (44.3%) were found to be victims of sexual abuse. Similarly, 60 per cent of the females were victims of physical abuse compared to only 44.9 per cent of the males. The females had a greater mean number of sexual abusers (4.5) compared to the males (1.4); were abused at an earlier age (64% before the age of 5 years) compared to the males (26% before 5 years of age); and were more likely to have been abused by both men and women (38%) compared to males (7%). Mathews *et al.* (1997) also reported that half the females in their sample met the clinical criteria for a diagnosis of PTSD.

These findings are consistent with those of Hickey *et al.* (2008) who, in the largest UK study of its kind, reported that, although male and female juveniles commit very similar patterns of HSB, their pathways to the behaviour appear to differ with respect to their experiences of childhood sexual abuse. Specifically, females presenting with HSB are not only more likely to be sexually victimised (96% females; 70% males), and at an earlier age (mean age females: 4 years; mean age males: 7 years), but they tend to be victimised by a more diverse and greater number of abusers (mean number of abusers, females: 3.5; mean number of abusers, males: 1). In addition, they are more likely to experience environments with poorer sexual boundaries. This general pattern is consistent with the higher levels of childhood sexual abuse in non-sexually abusing female juvenile delinquents (Lader, Singleton and Meltzer, 2003).

In summary, it appears that female juveniles who sexually abuse are more likely than males to have been victims of childhood sexual abuse and that abuse tends to be more severe, characterised by a greater number of abusers, a broader variety of abusers and an onset of abuse at an earlier age.

Treatment of young people with harmful sexual behaviour

A review of research into treatment for young people with HSB indicates that we are far from being able to draw firm conclusions about which approaches are most effective. CBT, Multi-Systemic Therapy (MST), psycho-educational models and family systemic work are all models that have been studied to varying degrees.

A systematic review by MacKenzie (2006) included a meta-analysis of seven studies that had a CBT approach alongside other treatments, including MST. While some evidence was presented for the effectiveness of CBT and MST there were serious limitations in relation to some sample sizes (which were small) and how the study effects were combined. Littell, Popa and Forsythe (2005) focused specifically on MST as a treatment for several kinds of behaviour; one of the eight studies included was an MST intervention for juveniles with harmful sexual behaviour. Again, because of a lack of consistency of results, and variation in the quality of the studies presented, it was concluded that it was premature to draw conclusions about the effectiveness of MST. Brooks-Gordon, Bilby and Wells (2006) conducted a systematic review of treatments for young people that sexually abuse that included one randomised control trial for CBT, 13 non-randomised trials and three qualitative studies. There was no significant evidence of treatment effect on recidivism and a general conclusion was drawn about the paucity of evidence for any treatment effectiveness from the current available data.

On a more positive note, several meta-analyses (as opposed to systematic reviews) have reported positive outcomes (in terms of reduced recidivism) in relation to treatment compared to comparison groups. Reitzel and Carbonell (2006) for example included nine treatment studies and reported an average weighted treatment effect size of 0.43 (CI=0.33–0.55). Other studies have reported similarly positive effects (Losel and Schmucker, 2005; Walker *et al.*, 2004). It remains unclear, however, which treatments are most associated with significant therapeutic change.

The number of treatment services and programmes in the UK has increased in recent years in the context of a community of practitioners dedicated to developing a coherent and clinically effective theoretical framework. As Hackett and colleagues (2006) describe in their review, many programmes employ cognitive behaviour approaches which usually address several of the following treatment elements: decreasing cognitive distortions; increasing empathy; enhancing problem solving skills; decreasing deviant sexual arousal; developing age appropriate social skills; resolving traumatic consequences of prior abuse; and enhancing management of emotions, mainly anger. There is also an increasing emphasis on recognising the importance of holistic and developmental goals as well as addressing HSB-specific issues (Hackett, 2004; Hackett *et al.*, 2006).

Marshall (2005) has highlighted the importance of enhancing hope, increasing self-esteem, and working collaboratively. He has suggested a move away from an exclusive focus on risk and relapse prevention that may lead to poor engagement and feelings of disempowerment and towards an increased focus on increasing an individual's capabilities, interests and skills to help them find more adaptive ways to meet their goals. This consideration is pertinent when one considers what we know about drop-out in the context of recidivism. In one meta-analysis of treatment effects for sex offenders (both juvenile and adult) completion of a programme of therapy doubled the likelihood of reduced recidivism compared with those who dropped out of treatment (Losel and Schmucker, 2005). Our manual with its subtitle *Change for Good* takes account of these factors by ensuring that the therapy addresses a range of developmental domains (not simply HSB) in the context of a positive, collaborative and goal focused framework.

Chapter 3

Preparing for Intervention

PRIOR ASSESSMENT

This manual aims to provide the clinician with a range of clinical materials for individual treatment and as such presupposes that any adolescent offered this intervention will have already received an adequate assessment. A detailed account of how to conduct such an assessment is beyond the scope of this book; however, some general principles are outlined below and in the box overleaf which summarises a set of core domains relevant for any assessment of HSB.

A comprehensive clinical assessment will gather information from a range of sources reflecting the different systems within which the child is embedded. These will include the birth family (parents, step parents and siblings), foster carers (and other children living in their care), the school system and peer relationships. Sourcing material from existing reports as well as through face-to-face meetings is essential to allow a comprehensive and accurate picture of risk and client need to be established (Print, Morrison and Henniker, 2001; Vizard 2002; Vizard, *et al.* 1996).

There are several models of assessment described in the literature. The *Asset* assessment profile, published by the Youth Justice Board (2006), provides a general method of assessing sexual and non-sexual risks, needs and strengths. There are specific schedules within the *Asset* tool to assess risk of serious harm and vulnerability, emotional and mental health, attitudes to victims and offending, family relationships and educational needs. *Asset* is often used as a case management tool in YOT settings; further details about its application can be found in the *Assessment, Planning, Interventions and Supervision* source document (Youth Justice Board, 2008). These materials are all freely available to download from the Youth Justice Board website (www.yjb.gov.uk).

The most established assessment model in the UK in relation to sexually abusive behaviour is the AIM assessment model (Assessment, Intervention and Moving on; Print *et al.*, 2001). Four domains of assessment are covered including a young person's sexual behaviour, development, parents and carers and environment. The model is constructed so as to inform service need, placement decisions and risk. Both concerns and strengths are assessed and they are considered at three levels:

- *the individual*: such as behavioural problems or trauma vs. a willingness to engage
- *the family*: such as experience of maltreatment or poor parenting vs. good boundaries at home
- *the environment*: such as exclusion from school vs. a good job.

Information is collected (including via interviews) by two co-workers and this provides the basis for calculating numerical scores for strengths and concerns. The scores are then placed in an outcome matrix and translated into a judgement about the level of supervision required. The whole assessment process follows ten steps, beginning with a referral and ending in the presentation of a report to an inter-agency strategy meeting. The model has since been developed further in the form of AIM2 and has also undergone some preliminary evaluation (Griffin and Beech, 2004).

CORE DOMAINS RELEVANT TO HSB ASSESSMENT

CHILD PROTECTION

Are there any current child protection concerns? These might relate to contact with previous victims or possible future victims, as well as concerns about the welfare of the young person being assessed.

HSB

Detailing the known HSB, the nature of the victim, setting, use of planning and coercion and the young person's attitudes to their actions.

RISK

What is the level of risk of future HSB *and* anti-social behaviour? What factors are likely to increase and decrease risk?

STRENGTHS

What are the protective and resilience factors likely to work in the young person's favour? These might include supportive relationships, adaptive personal characteristics, good cognitive ability, a settled living situation, non-academic talents, to name but a few.

DEVELOPMENTAL HISTORY AND FAMILY CONTEXT

This may be obtained by a mixture of direct assessment as the review of existing records. Mapping out the family genogram and making explicit links about the nature of relationships between family members (noting in particular domestic violence, maltreatment and neglect). In addition the young person's own history of sexualised behaviour and response to previous interventions is important.

MENTAL HEALTH AND COGNITIVE FUNCTIONING

Not every professional will be adequately trained to complete a full mental health assessment. However, the clinician should at the very least screen for the presence of possible mental health problems. These commonly include the presence of conduct disorder, post-traumatic stress disorder (PTSD), attention-deficit hyperactivity disorder (ADHD), and speech and language problems. In addition, it is important to pick up any indications of a learning disability. Children are often adept at using social strategies to conceal underlying intellectual problems; if there is a concern, a properly trained psychologist should be asked to conduct a psychometric assessment.

Vizard (2002) also describes a multidisciplinary model of assessment developed within a four tier specialist assessment and treatment service (originally YAP, now known as the NSPCC NCATS service). This provides a detailed framework for psychological, psychiatric and risk issues to be assessed within a multidisciplinary context.

A new but yet to be validated assessment tool is the MEGA (Multiplex Empirically Guided Inventory of Ecological Aggregates for Assessing Sexually Abusive Adolescents and Children; Miccio-Fonseca 2009). MEGA reflects the current view that protective factors (such as engagement in treatment and positive parental relationships) should be considered alongside traditional risk-related indices.

Measuring risk

A number of measures aimed at providing an actuarial measure of the risk of offending which are derived from statistical probabilities observed in a population of young people with HSB are in the process of development. These contrast with clinical estimations of risk where experience and an individual formulation of a particular young person's behaviour based on a comprehensive assessment is used to estimate the probability of future HSB. In practice an actuarial measure only offers a general guide for assessing risk in an individual case (Worling, 2004); accuracy and relevance of the estimation depends on several factors including:

- quality and quantity of the information about an individual
- extent to which the individual shares those group characteristics of risk measured by the instrument
- reliability and validity of the instrument itself
- extent to which the instrument has been validated externally on the populations concerned.

The two main tools currently being developed are the Juvenile Sex Offender Assessment Protocol (J-SOAP) developed by Prentky and colleagues (2000) and the Estimate of Risk of Adolescent Sexual Offense Recidivism (ERASOR) developed by Worling and Curwen (2001). Both measures are designed to assess the historical static factors related to previous sexual offences and dynamic factors, such as sexual interest, pro-offending attitudes, social factors and self-management (Beech, Fisher and Thornton, 2003). Initial research has shown encouraging results but findings remain preliminary (Righthand *et al.*, 2005). Those who wish to explore further issues related to risk assessment are recommended the recent review published by Rich (2009).

PREPARING FOR THERAPY

Requirements for the clinician

There are several practical and logistical steps that should be taken before beginning any direct work with the young person. These include: arrangements for supervision; ensuring that child protection concerns are adequately addressed; and putting in place arrangements to allow effective communication between all the professionals involved in the young person's care. While only a brief description of each of these issues are described below, their importance should not be under-estimated. This manual primarily provides guidance regarding the direct work in the room with the young person; however, ensuring that an adequate systemic framework is in place at the beginning and indeed throughout the process of therapy is critical for the success of any therapeutic work with this client group.

Hawkes (2002) outlines the basic requirements for any clinician offering an individual treatment service to young people who have sexually abused. He highlights the importance of ensuring that there are clear child protection strategies in place with a policy of open-confidentiality requiring information regarding undisclosed child sexual abuse to be shared with the police, social services, and other relevant professionals. In addition he recommends that the clinician has access to other disciplines and works in a setting which is safe, with clear guidelines for ensuring that safety is maintained. As highlighted later there is also a need for adequate supervision to be provided, monitoring of work and access to ongoing training.

Addressing child protection concerns

Prior to therapy commencing it is necessary for any child protection concerns to be addressed. Current practice guidelines (Department of Health, 2006) reiterate that it is important for clinicians to recognise the potential for conflict between the welfare of a juvenile abuser and the welfare of their victim. Where this occurs, the victim's welfare should be paramount over that of the offender. In addition, current child protection guidelines should be consulted and followed in relation to the offender and the victim.

Certain elements of any intervention may at times serve to increase risk (for example, by heightening levels of sexual arousal) and this should be closely monitored in liaison with other professionals involved in the care of the young person, including, for example, their social worker, carer and, where appropriate, teacher. A young person in treatment should ideally be in a stable placement where their level of risk is being monitored. In our view, at minimum there should be a good likelihood that the young person will remain in the same placement for the duration of the treatment. In cases where contact has been permitted, the young person would not be expected to have unsupervised time with their victim until treatment has been shown to be effective.

Coordination between professionals

The needs of young people with HSB often cut across social, educational and youth justice provision. As with assessment, an effective treatment programme will only take place in a framework of partnership between professionals and agencies who are liaising on the basis of a joint understanding of the problems being addressed and the aims of treatment. It is typically recommended that there is a lead professional responsible for coordinating the assessment and treatment intervention for a given young person. In order for a shared understanding of intervention to be agreed there needs to be clarity among the professionals involved as to the aims and structure of a treatment package. The following factors are important and could be shared between workers as guidelines to ensure this occurs:

- *Hold a preliminary professionals meeting.* This is a meeting with all relevant professionals prior to the beginning of therapy – it can be particularly helpful to ensure that there is support and engagement from the professional network and that the young person in treatment receives consistent and coherent messages. At a minimum, this group should include a representative from the young person's school, their social worker, a professional representing criminal justice provision (if relevant) and the clinician. A follow-up letter outlining the therapy plan to all concerned is recommended.

- *Circulate dates of all meetings before, during and after treatment.* Such planning helps facilitate a systemic approach and involves other colleagues directly in a supportive role. If difficulties arise during the course of the intervention then such links are likely to become particularly important. Meetings with the young person's carer (foster carer or parent) also need to be considered, as well as their role in supporting the young person in treatment. These should always form part of the treatment package, but will vary in number and structure depending on each case. More discussion on working with the parents or carers of a young person in treatment is provided in Chapter 4.

- *Maintain a confidentiality agreement.* Clear arrangements about information sharing, confidentiality and management of risk should all be agreed in advance. These are there to facilitate feedback from the clinician if concerns arise and effective management of risk both for the young person in treatment and for other children and young people. It can be helpful for a protocol to be in place to allow the clinician to receive a regular update prior to each clinical session regarding any problems or risk situations that have arisen over the previous week.

- *Set up escort arrangements for the young person.* Depending on the setting, the clinician delivering the intervention, the age of the young person and their estimated level of risk, appropriate arrangements need to be made to ensure they are escorted safely to their weekly session(s). These arrangements need to be in place and agreed before intervention is offered.

- *Develop a preliminary treatment formulation and treatment plan.* On the basis of the assessment, a preliminary treatment formulation and treatment plan should be written prior to the intervention outlining the number and nature of the sessions that are to be offered. This of course may be open to later revision.

- *Identify an appropriate therapeutic venue.* For most therapeutic work with children it is recommended that therapy take place in a quiet private room. However, for this group of young people with harmful sexual behaviour, there needs to be a balance with the risk posed to the clinician(s) in terms of acting out, aggression and even false allegations. This is likely to be particularly true for young people who have a history of posing threats to adults or who are in custodial or mental health residential settings. In these cases of higher risk a door with observation panels, or live supervision via video link, may be warranted. Ideally, the same room should be used over the course of the intervention; if this is not possible, some continuity of the room used for each module would be preferable. This continuity helps provide a sense of security and safety, and works to build the therapeutic rapport. Good organisation will ensure that rooms are booked in advance and correctly set up. Two chairs diagonally arranged, and a small table, are all the furniture that is required; excess chairs should be neatly set to one side. A flip-chart, plenty of spare paper and different coloured pens are also essential materials to many of the sessions in this manual.

Together, these arrangements will help ensure the safety of the clinician as well as the young person. Once adequate arrangements are in place in each domain then direct work can begin. The first step for the clinician is to consider the specific aims of the intervention and relate these to a treatment formulation of the young person's presenting difficulties. This is addressed in the following chapter.

Chapter 4

Delivering the Intervention

THE AIMS OF INTERVENTION

A core challenge when delivering an effective intervention for this group of adolescents is to balance a focus on harmful sexual behaviours with a broader set of clinical priorities aimed at addressing other problem behaviours and promoting better psycho-social functioning. Each young person will have their own profile of needs, vulnerabilities and strengths, which will require the clinician to tailor any therapy appropriately. One can think about an intervention for HSB as having two very broad aims.

1. **First, the treatment should aim to increase the likelihood that a young person will show sexual and non-sexual behaviours that are socially acceptable and refrain from harmful sexual behaviour.** This aim articulates the need to eliminate abusive and harmful behaviours and at the same time helps the adolescent cultivate alternative and acceptable behaviours.

2. **Second, the treatment should aim to enhance psycho-social functioning, increasing the young person's sense of optimism about the future and their current sense of wellbeing.** This more holistic goal seeks to reduce risk and increase the likelihood of a positive trajectory for the adolescent by enhancing their ability to attain future goals.

When delivering the therapy in the room it can be helpful to articulate these aims in a way that creates a shared sense of purpose; this can be particularly helpful for the young person (and clinician) when it feels that the focus of the work is starting to drift. In the language accessible to the young person and from their perspective the aims might be reframed as:

1. *To not sexually harm others and to have healthy sexual relationships as an adult.*

2. *To handle problems well and feel good about myself.*

Rich (2003, p.244) operationalised the 17 specific treatment areas originally recommended by the National Task Force on Juvenile Sexual Offending (1993) in the United States into nine concrete objectives. These objectives related to a range of domains including sexual behaviour as well as more generic aspects of functioning; together these required the young person to:

1. identify and address the constellation of thoughts, feelings, beliefs and behaviours that are directly related to their abuse

2. develop responsibility for behaviour while being mindful of the risk of minimisation or inappropriate justification

3. be helped to process the impact of past trauma

4. work to become more aware and sensitive to the needs of others

5. become adequately informed regarding what constitutes normative and deviant sexual development

6. develop strategies to identify and challenge deviant sexual arousal and fantasy

7. develop their coping and social skills

8. work towards more adaptive relationships

9. develop and be able to implement an effective relapse prevention plan.

As treatment aspirations these aims are relevant and appropriate. The reality, however, is that as clinicians we are only able to partially shift an adolescent along each of these dimensions. For example, it is rare that any adolescent (or indeed adult) is fully able to take responsibility for behaviours about which they feel ashamed or which they believe were justified given the unfair behaviour of others. Similarly, for those young people with greater levels of callous-unemotional traits (see Chapter 2), it may be an impossible task within a time limited therapeutic intervention to foster a genuine compassion for others. These caveats are noted here not to diminish the importance of aspiring to these aims, but rather to acknowledge that they are ideals and falling short from them should not lead a clinician to feel dispirited or resigned. Change in each dimension, no matter how limited, represents positive and meaningful progress. In the context of what we know about the deprived and abusive experiences of many young people with HSB it is not surprising that they will find it difficult to internalise responsibility and consideration for others given that they have, in all likelihood, had limited exposure themselves to such behaviours. Clinicians should therefore be realistic and at the same time optimistic in their efforts and expectations of engendering change.

DEVELOPING A TREATMENT FORMULATION

As outlined in Chapter 3, all adolescents entering treatment should already have received a comprehensive assessment leading to an assessment report. Typically this assessment would include a formulation of the offence behaviour, an estimation of risk and recommendations for intervention. The clinician delivering the intervention may or may not have been part of the original assessment team.

Prior to commencing the manual's *Change for Good* programme the treating clinician, whether involved in the original assessment or not, should develop, on the basis of the assessment report and information from other available sources, a preliminary *treatment formulation*. Formulation plays an important role in many therapeutic models. Here, we use treatment formulation to refer to an explanatory model, which makes sense of the young person's HSB (and any offending behaviour) within the context of their life experiences and internal world. Note that the treatment formulation is a set of hypotheses (in other words, it is not the 'truth' but rather the clinician's best guess at understanding the problem), and as such it is open to change and adjustment as treatment progresses. It is also not the same as an estimation of risk, which is more about the future than making sense of the past. That said, a treatment formulation can be helpful in thinking about future risk.

A schematic treatment formulation template, designed specifically for use with this manual, is provided below (see Figure 4.1). Figure 4.2 provides a worked example. This template can act as a simple framework to bring together disparate elements of information that are relevant to piecing together an explanatory model of what might have contributed to the young person's harmful sexual behaviour. The template comprises a number of components, some dynamic and some historical, including the following:

Predisposing factors

These can relate to relevant historical factors (e.g. parental marital breakdown, experience of sexual abuse, witnessing domestic violence, being scapegoated) that the young person experienced. It may not become clear until the intervention is underway which of these is most salient.

Attachment and behavioural problems

Here the clinician should consider stability of placement, contact with primary caregivers, contact with individuals the young person regards as trusted adults, experience of rejection, peer relationships and so forth. It is important to ensure that positive as well as negative attachment experiences are noted. In addition, it is useful to describe here other behaviour problems that are manifest.

Predisposing factors

Attachment and behaviour problems

FAMILY

PEERS

Beliefs

SELF

WORLD

FUTURE

PRECIPITATING FACTORS

HSB

UNMET GOALS

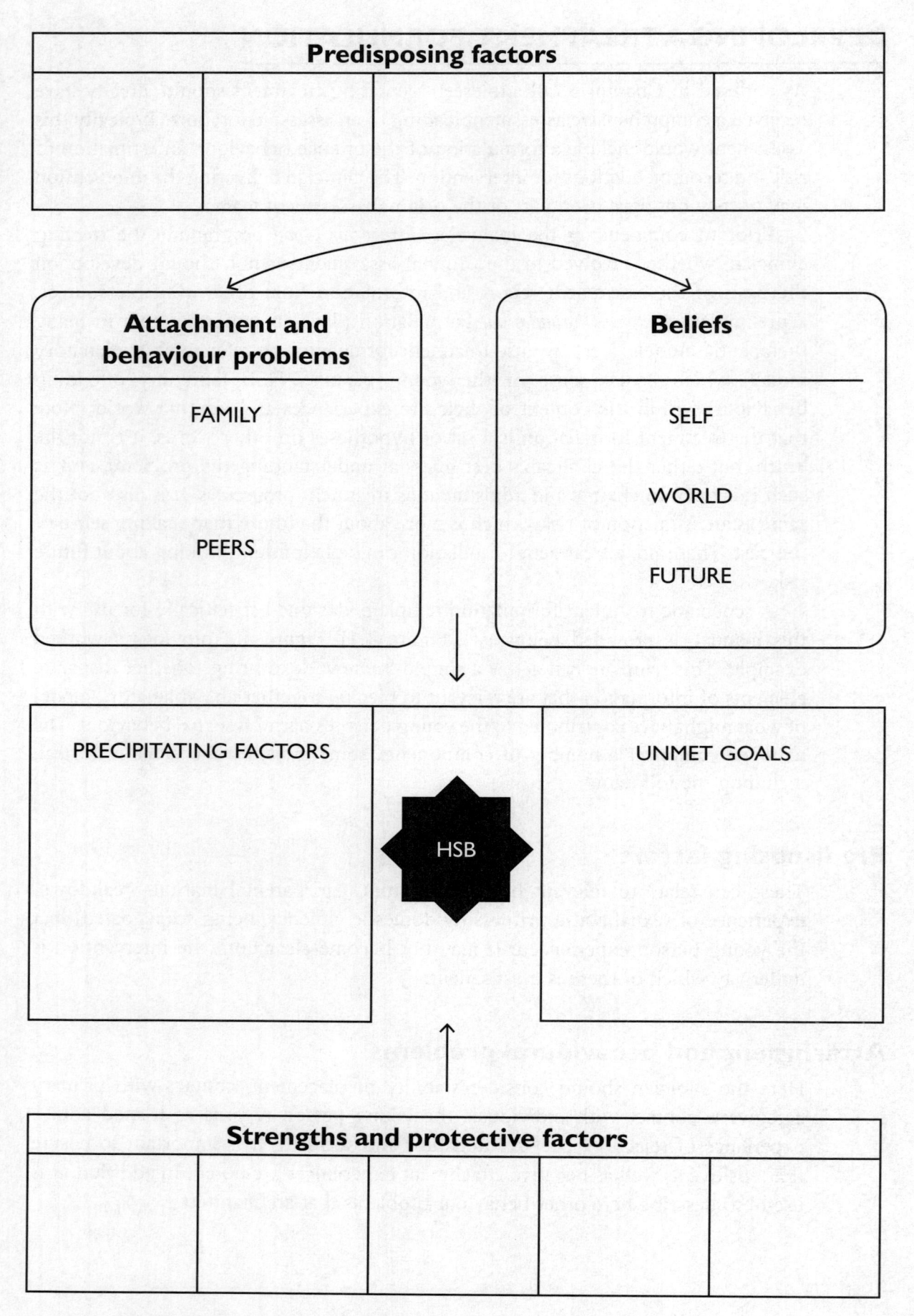

Strengths and protective factors

Figure 4.1 Treatment formulation template

Predisposing factors				
Pre-term birth	Poor sexual boundaries at home	Domestic violence	Early seperation from father	4 placement changes in 2 years

Attachment and behaviour problems

FAMILY
Anger towards mother
Erratic contact with father
Idolisation of father
Withdrawal from current carers

PEERS
Social isolation – no 'good' friends
Aggressive episodes at school – fights

Beliefs

SELF
'I am unlovable'

WORLD
'No one really cares'
'I am goingto pay people back'

FUTURE
'Nothing is going to work out – there is no point even trying'

PRECIPITATING FACTORS

Marriage of mother to step-father who has two children of his own – felt excluded and rejected

Moving schools

HSB

UNMET GOALS

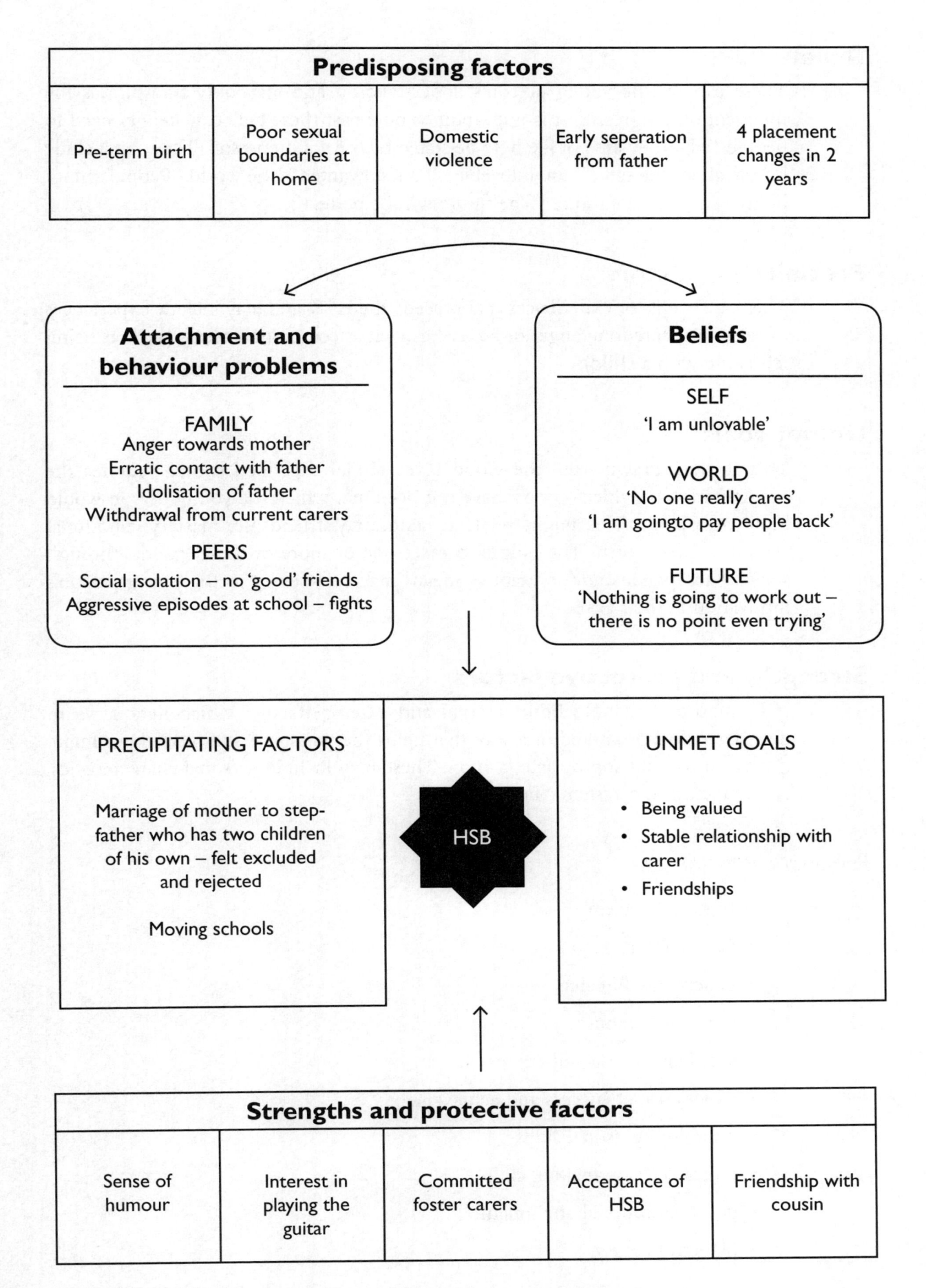

- Being valued
- Stable relationship with carer
- Friendships

Strengths and protective factors				
Sense of humour	Interest in playing the guitar	Committed foster carers	Acceptance of HSB	Friendship with cousin

Figure 4.2 Treatment formulation template – worked example

Beliefs

These capture the young person's understanding and may only transpire as the intervention progresses. It is important to note that these beliefs generally need to be inferred – they are not likely to be stated by the young person. They can include beliefs about the self ('I am unlovable'; 'I am unwanted'), the world ('People cannot be trusted') and the future ('The future will be perfect').

Precipitating factors

These are events or experiences that precede the HSB, and may include experiences of rejection, boredom, anger or arousal as well as contextual factors (such as being left alone with a child).

Unmet goals

This section, drawn from the Good Lives model described earlier, requires the consideration of which 'goods' have not been met which the young person would aspire to obtain. This might relate to autonomy, friendship, mastery, emotional stability and so forth. The failure to meet one or more of these 'goods' through socially acceptable and/or adaptive means may be relevant to the young person's motivation in their HSB.

Strengths and protective factors

It is important to note both internal and external factors which may serve to decrease risk if promoted in a way that helps the young person meet their unmet goals in a socially appropriate fashion. These may include personal characteristics, family factors and systemic factors.

Personal characteristics

- high self-esteem
- verbal ability
- general intelligence
- sense of humour
- problem solving skills
- experience of success and achievement
- good interpersonal skills
- moral decision making skills
- good educational attainment
- planning ability.

Family factors

- family cohesion or harmony
- close bond with at least one person
- absence of parental mental health problems or addictions
- sibling attachment
- family or placement stability
- trust.

Systemic factors

- good peer relationships
- good school experience
- presence of positive role models
- supports external to the family.

An example of a worked treatment formulation is provided in Figure 4.2.

It is recommended that a preliminary treatment formulation, based on the assessment information, is developed prior to seeing the young person for the first time. This preliminary treatment formulation should be revisited and amended on the basis of the clinician's experience of the young person in treatment and the material they present with; this iterative process is shown in Figure 4.3, 'Overview of the treatment process'. It would be very surprising if, as the intervention progressed, a clinician did not develop and modify their understanding of the young person's behaviour and how it related to early experiences and the adolescent's current thoughts, feelings, beliefs and behaviours. The treatment formulation should not act as a burden – rather it should foster an ongoing curiosity and exploration of why the young person thinks and acts as they do and provide a guide for the clinician in how they focus the work of each session. Often what might look like an important factor may transpire to be of little relevance as the formulation is developed.

OVERARCHING GOALS OF TREATMENT

The broad treatment aims described above can be usefully broken down into more concrete treatment goals or tasks. Thinking explicitly about the core tasks that comprise the intervention makes it easier for the clinician to modify and tailor their work depending on the needs of the individual young person in treatment. In reality, however, such tasks are typically overlapping and intertwined. We first outline two overarching goals essential to an effective intervention; we then break down the treatment work into ten more specific treatment goals or areas. How these areas are addressed at different stages of the intervention is illustrated in Figure 4.4.

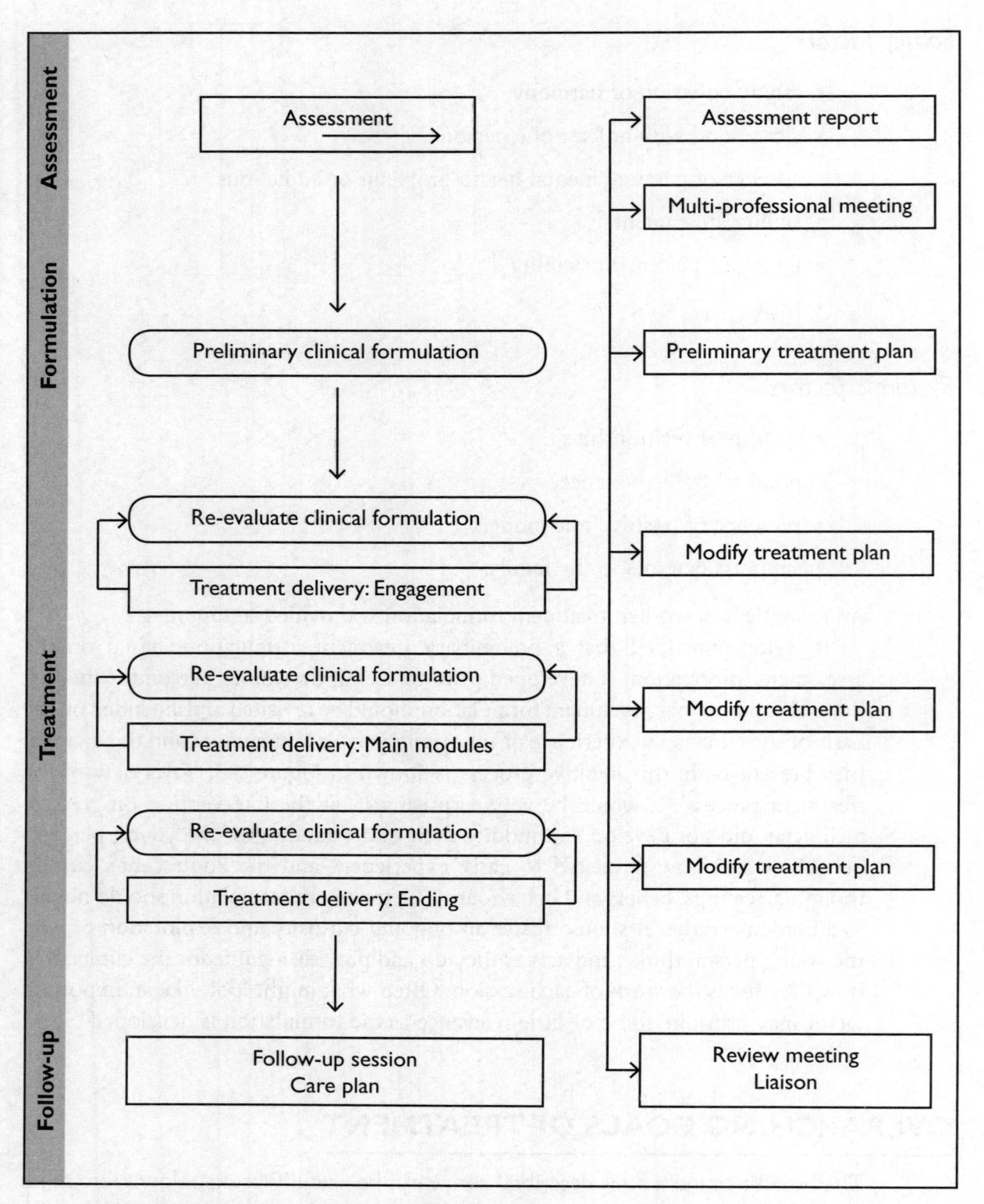

Figure 4.3 Overview of the treatment process

		Core Treatment Tasks									
Module/Session No.	Building positive treatment alliance and systemic support	Positive future vision	Positive self-narrative	Relationships	Managing anger	Insight: Impact of HSB on self	Insight: Impact of HSB on victim	Mentalisation ability	Understanding/ managing HSB	Taking responsibility	Healthy vs. HSB
Engagement											
1		•									
2		•					•				
3		•	•	•							
4		•	•								
Relationships		Developing adaptive relationship skills									
1		•		•							
2				•	•			•			
3				•	•			•			
4			•						•	•	
5			•						•		•
6				•			•	•	•		
7		•		•		•	•				
8				•	•						
9				•		•			•		•
Self-Regulation		Strategies to manage sexual behaviour problems and anger									
1				•	•			•			
2				•	•			•			•
3						•			•		•
4			•			•					
5			•			•	•		•	•	
6								•	•	•	
7				•					•		
8				•	•			•			
Road Map		Future relationships and relapse prevention planning									
1, 2		•		•					•		•
3, 4, 5		•	•	•	•	•	•	•	•	•	•

Figure 4.4 Core treatment objectives mapped across sessions

Overarching Goal 1: Building a positive therapeutic alliance

The role played by the client-therapist relationship is now well recognised across the range of psychotherapies for adults and children (see for example Ackerman and Hilsenroth, 2003; Eltz *et al.* 1995). According to Lambert (1992), the therapeutic alliance accounts for 30 per cent of the variance in treatment outcome – irrespective of what form of therapy is delivered. However, cultivating a sound therapeutic alliance with this client group can be challenging in several respects. First, as we have seen, many young people with HSB have experienced unstable and (for some) abusive relationships from an early age. These experiences increase the likelihood of poorer interpersonal skills and greater wariness in trusting an unknown adult. Second, like many of their peers during adolescence, these young people may tend to define themselves by opposing established authority structures (e.g. parents, school, police) and clinicians can easily find themselves perceived as an authority figure. Third, working with clients who generally are both victims and perpetrators can elicit complex and contradictory feelings in clinicians, of for example sympathy, anger, revulsion or confusion, which, if not managed effectively, can negatively impact on the therapeutic alliance.

The task for the clinician, therefore, is to cultivate a positive therapeutic alliance while at the same time to challenge in appropriate thoughts or behaviours that might harm the client or another person. In other words, it is neither ethical nor consistent with the aims of treatment to 'go along' with anything unacceptable the adolescent might think or do in the interests of maintaining an alliance.

What is required is a therapeutic stance towards the young person that is:

- caring and empathic
- honest and authentic
- reliable and trustworthy
- accepting of them as an individual who is valued and deserving of respect,

but which, *at the same time*:

- invites responsibility
- is honest and clear about what are socially acceptable (and indeed legal) boundaries
- challenges unacceptable beliefs and behaviour
- is confident and assured.

Combining both sets of qualities forms the bedrock of a successful therapeutic alliance with this client group. As will be discussed later a number of practical techniques can be helpful in achieving this. For example, presenting views that are contrary to those of the adolescent in a straightforward and emotionally neutral way, rather than in a lecturing or patronising tone, sets the context for reflection and a balanced discussion rather than disagreement. Establishing a good therapeutic alliance can also be understood as providing a safe context where a consistent and reliable attachment can be formed with the clinician, which in turn increases the potential for reflection and cognitive change. Thus, establishing an effective alliance is not (as it can sometimes appear) incompatible with challenging the young person and asking difficult questions. Rather it is precisely a solid collaborative alliance that allows difficult material to be worked with on an ongoing basis.

Overarching Goal 2: Building systemic support

If the young person is going to develop new patterns of behaviour and new ways of thinking about themselves and others then it is important that there are concurrent changes in their social environment. These changes both facilitate change within the therapy and serve as a key protective factor once therapy has ended. The clinician should aim to promote and facilitate the support network available to the young person and work to shift attitudes or behaviours in others that are serving to block change. For example, the clinician may:

- *Help the adolescent develop appropriate peer-age friendships.* Some young people with HSB are particularly socially isolated and lack the skills to make and keep friends. This in turn can limit their access to normal adolescent social activities and interests. Encouraging the young person to develop their social skills and peer network can reap important benefits allowing them to develop new interests, a sense of autonomy and personal competence.

- *Work with the young person's school or college to ensure that they are not permanently excluded from education.* Some schools will choose not to accept young people with HSB but most are amenable to working with a clinical team who can help them develop and implement a risk management strategy that will allow the adolescent to benefit from ongoing access to education. Over the course of intervention this strategy may be modified in order to give the young person more autonomy if they have demonstrated a capacity to be trusted. The goal is to help the young person to develop an *internalised* set of beliefs and skills that will allow them to regulate their own behaviour in an acceptable way; if they are deprived of new (albeit carefully controlled) opportunities to develop then, once external constraints are lifted, their level of risk may have not actually have changed.

- *Help the young person find work if they are not in education.* For example, in the Relationships module, the clinician rather than focusing on parental relationships may choose to focus on role-plays related to job interviews. Such a focus can emerge naturally from the weekly feedback discussion with the young person alongside thinking about their future aspirations.

- *Work closely with team members who are helping the parents manage and support their child over the course of the intervention programme.* Later we describe some of the issues that arise when working with parents or carers of adolescents in treatment for HSB. Some parents need help in shifting their understanding and behaviour towards the young person in their care. Their behaviours can at times be overly punitive and restrictive and at other times demonstrate a lack of awareness of risk and an inconsistency in maintaining boundaries. An ongoing dialogue between the clinician and the professionals working with the parents can be very helpful.

The work to develop a young person's support network should always be conducted in a child protection context. For example, it would not be appropriate to encourage a young person (with a history of abusing younger children) to join a swimming club known to have younger members. If such a development emerges during the young person's weekly feedback for example, it would be essential to feed this information back after the session to their social worker. At the same time, the clinician may need to play a role in working with other professionals to ensure that punitive (and ultimately counter-productive) sanctions are not imposed in order to reduce perceived risk. Such collaborative working with carers and professionals is likely to vary across cases, but in all instances can provide a genuine context for learning and growth – in other words, real opportunities for the young person to develop outside as well as inside the therapy room.

THE DELIVERY OF A TYPICAL SESSION

Preparation prior to a session

Before delivering the intervention it is assumed that the clinician will be familiar with the issues outlined in this introduction and with the overall content of the manual and CD-ROM's *Change for Good* programme. Prior to any given session it is recommended that the clinician:

- is familiar with the session plan
- completes the session preparation sheet – this should outline the main tasks of the session notes about possible issues that may arise or issues that the clinician may wish to raise in the light of previous work
- ensures that all clinical notes are up to date
- is aware if there have been any incidents or concerns that have arisen since the previous session
- takes a view regarding the feasibility and relevance of covering the material outlined in the session plan – for example, they may choose to split the material over more than one session or focus on one task that is of particular relevance to the young person in treatment.

Delivery of a typical session

While the content of a typical session is likely to vary it is envisaged that for this programme its overall structure should remain relatively stable. Each session is essentially divided into the following stages.

1. Weekly review – Setting the agenda – Home project

This introductory phase should be tightly organised so not to derail the session; typically it should not exceed the first 15 minutes and on average should take only 10 minutes. The weekly review provides an opportunity to briefly explore with the young person how they have found the previous week. Any salient issues that arise or concerns that they wish to discuss should be noted and placed on the agenda to be discussed in the *Issues to discuss* section. For example, the clinician might say:

> '*It sounds like you were quite annoyed at not being able to go into town on Saturday and ended up having an argument with your mum, is that right? Do you think this is something we should spend some time thinking about? ... Okay, let's put it on our agenda and we will come back to it later in the session.*'

Setting the agenda follows the same structure each week and once the young person is familiar with the process it can proceed quite quickly. It is a chance to introduce the tasks that a given session will focus on, but also a chance to check with the young person whether they have issues they wish to discuss, or preferences on how the session will be focused: '*How does that sound? Is there anything you would like to add?*' A balance needs to be struck between becoming overly reactive to the ideas introduced by the young person and maintaining a degree of structure and adherence to what has been planned. The clinician may (and should) judge that it is necessary to deviate from the agenda and explore an issue that seems relevant and of importance for the young person and that is okay. The agenda should be seen as a flexible framework that promotes a good use of clinical time, not a straightjacket that limits appropriate clinical exploration.

Finally, in this introductory section the clinician should review the young person's home project. Some guidance on this is provided in the individual session plans. In general a review of the home project should be concise and involve obtaining feedback from the young person: '*How did you find this week's home project? What did you find easy/difficult? What did you learn?*' Ideally the clinician should make links between the content of the home project and work that has been completed in previous sessions or events that have taken place at home or at school. It is important to reinforce successful completion of homework with specific praise.

2. Task completion

Every session plan contains one or two tasks that represent the main material to be covered in the session. How these are structured varies a great deal. The clinician should use their discretion in deciding which aspects of a task should be emphasised (there is generally more material to cover than time) depending on the treatment formulation for a given young person at that time. Actively engaging the young person in the task (rather than talking 'at' them) and inviting them to contribute using the flip-chart should be common features of every task. As noted earlier the clinician may choose to split the material over more than one session.

3. Issues to discuss

This is a dedicated space in the session where issues or concerns that have arisen either at the beginning of the session, or while completing the tasks, can have a space to be explored. Depending on how much there is to cover, this section should begin 10 to 15 minutes before the end of the session. Having this more open section after the tasks are completed means that it is more likely to be contained and less likely to derail the focus of the session.

4. Summary and home project

It can be useful to end the session with a brief summary statement about what was covered. The clinician should be familiar with the home project so that they can provide a ready explanation to the young person and answer any queries they have.

5. Feedback

Rather than the clinician providing feedback from their point of view, it is better to ask the young person how they found the session. This helps them reflect and consolidate insights that they may have gained. Specific feedback questions are normally best; for example: '*Tell me one thing that you learnt from today's session*' or '*Tell me one good thing and one difficult thing about today's session*'

NOTE

In the descriptions of individual sessions, there are lots of examples of what the clinician might say, which are italicised. These examples should not be taken literally but are offered as suggestions that should be adapted. The exact words are not critical.

Tasks after a session is completed

Following each session the clinician should write a summary of the session. Typically this will include some description of the content and the themes arising, but also something about *how* the young person presented and the dynamics or quality of their interaction.

Any child protection concerns that arise in the session should be noted and communicated as necessary to the young person's social worker and other relevant professionals.

WORKING IN THE ROOM: TEN CORE TREATMENT COMPONENTS

1. Positive future vision

A core tool used within the *Change for Good* intervention is that of the visual timeline. This is particularly important in the early stages. The timeline, developed collaboratively with the young person on two large pieces of paper, acts as a concrete forum for them to elaborate a positive vision of their future: where they would like to be, who they would like to be with and what they would like to be doing. This positive vision can act as a powerful motivator for change as it provides a set of goals and aspirations that are incompatible with ongoing HSB. For some young people with entrenched and longstanding sexual behaviour problems the future can be rather sparsely defined; it is the role of the clinician to help them elaborate a positive vision of the future and create a sense of what a successful future might actually look like. The timeline is also used to capture past experiences and the future negative consequences of ongoing HSB as discussed below.

2. Positive self-narrative

A second aim is to help the young person develop a more positive self-concept relating both to their past and to their future. At an explicit level this narrative is a verbalised 'story' which makes sense of their past experiences and creates a sense of their identity for the future. Given the past victimisation and attachment instability of many young people displaying HSB, the past can often be represented in a fragmented way, with salient emotive events poorly integrated with a broader sense of their lives and development. Typically there are past and current feelings of rejection, injustice, fear and uncertainty relating to family relationships and to the *absence* of relationships (perhaps a father, or father figure). Underlying beliefs, about the self (e.g. as being unlovable, inadequate, unwanted), the world (e.g. as being unpredictable, threatening, rejecting) and the future (e.g. as sometimes negative, and sometimes over-idealised and distorted), inform the young person's narrative which can be an attempt to protect themselves against the pain of their own experience of not being valued.

A running thread throughout the intervention is to help the young person to articulate and develop their narrative. For the clinician, it is important to be curious about what gets left out of the narrative as it is likely that components may be omitted because they are dissonant with dominant negative beliefs about the self. For example, the young person may have had 'a grandmother who loved me' or 'a teacher who was interested in me' but fails to spontaneously recall these in describing their past relationships. The use of the visual timeline, which is placed on the wall during every session, is one practical tool that can help achieve a balanced picture of the young person's past. Part of this work is to also articulate the harmful behaviour they showed in the past. Together, these elements should form a more balanced self-narrative, the aim of which is for the young person to:

- develop a sense of coherence about events in their life
- outline their role and responsibility for things that have happened
- accord due responsibility to others (who may have failed to care for them)
- articulate their feelings about their past
- identify past strengths and successes
- describe future aspirations – both in terms of who they wish to be (internal goals) and what they wish to do (external goals).

Helping the young person to think about their future, and how they would like things to be different, can provide useful leverage in eliciting motivation to change; a key question the clinician can ask in this respect is: '*If that is where you want to be, what needs to be different?*'

3. Relationships

Harmful sexual behaviour profoundly transgresses emotional, physical and social boundaries and is typically associated with a wider clinical phenotype of relationship deficits. In fact, many adolescents with HSB present with this behaviour precisely because they have failed to develop or internalise age-appropriate relationship skills; this can lead to social isolation from peers or manifest in the context of fractured and conflictual family relationships. The domain of relationships clearly spans an extremely wide area; within the Relationships module three main areas are covered:

1. *Relationship boundaries:* helping the young person to internalise what constitutes appropriate and inappropriate behaviour in different contexts, particularly in relation to sexual behaviour.

2. *Mentalisation skills:* helping the young person to think and reflect about other people's thoughts, feelings and intentions, particularly those of their victim; this important task is discussed in more detail in a separate section.

3. *Relationship skills:* assisting the young person in being able to communicate their needs effectively especially in managing disagreements so that they do not escalate into aggression or harmful behaviour.

In order to provide some thematic consistency to each module the Relationships module predominantly focuses on interpersonal aspects – external features of a young person's interactions with others – while the Self-Regulation module predominantly focuses on internal aspects of their own mental life and emotional experience.

A number of vignettes are provided in the Relationships module to encourage the young person to think about what features are core to any good relationship; these are sometimes role-played in order to help develop practical skills in dealing with relationship difficulties, for example managing a disagreement or saying no to sex. Throughout the module this more tangential focus should be shifted by the clinician to directly think about the adolescent's *own* relationships, both positive and negative. The relationship with the clinician can itself act as one important opportunity for the young person to develop a relationship characterised by mutual respect, trust and appropriate boundaries.

4. Managing anger

Many, but not all, young people with HSB have problems in managing their anger. This can manifest in non-sexual physical and verbal aggression towards others, including peers, siblings, teachers and carers. Studies of the adolescent brain suggest that during this developmental period there is likely to be a heightening of subjective emotional experience in the absence of a fully matured capacity for effective emotional regulation (see Chapter 2). We know from research in the field of general delinquency that the majority of criminal offences are committed by males during adolescence and young adulthood. It is postulated that this highly significant trend may be due to a combination of neuro-psychological deficits and environmental adversity in some adolescents and a maladaptive attempt to gain adult status in others (Moffitt, 1993; 2006).

While it is the case that childhood experiences of maltreatment are likely to be associated with exposure to violent behaviour and deficits in self-regulation they are also likely to lead to a sense of simply not being valued. The experience of not being cared for and thought about by adults understandably leaves many children feeling angry and disappointed; in such cases destructive patterns of aggression are more easily triggered by everyday experiences of (perceived or real) rejection or conflict. Yet for some children aggression is one way to regain a sense of power and control and banish (at least temporarily) feelings of insecurity and vulnerability.

Such non-sexual aggression is not always evident in adolescents presenting with HSB and the clinician should modify the focus of their work accordingly if it does not seem relevant to their treatment formulation. Of equal importance, however, is the role of aggression as part of the HSB. It is not uncommon for an incident of harmful sexual behaviour to be preceded by an experience of rejection, which elicits strong feelings of anger. The HSB can act as a strategy to manage these feelings – a young person may punish another to project (and therefore partly neutralise) painful feelings of being punished themselves and exert power in the form of sexual aggression in order to negate profound feelings of worthlessness.

Several ways of helping the young person to manage anger are provided across sessions in both the Relationships and Self-Regulation modules. These relate to:

- helping the young people develop a more positive view of themselves by working on their self-narrative
- acknowledging the genuine injustices that they may have themselves experienced by not being adequately cared for by adults
- helping them develop a greater awareness of when and how angry feelings arise
- providing practical adaptive strategies to manage feelings of anger as alternatives to aggression.

5. Insight: Impact of HSB on self

The visual timeline is used not only to help the young person construct a positive vision of their future, but also to contrast that positive trajectory with the consequences for themselves if they continue to sexually harm others. Session 7 in the Relationships module in fact explicitly explores with the young person the consequences of a repeated episode of HSB on their own future. The aim is to create a tangible sense of consequences in both the short term (e.g. being removed from home) and longer term (e.g. going to prison and being denied work and study opportunities). These are mapped onto the timeline in order to give a real sense of the choice that faces them when they have thoughts and feelings about sexually abusing again.

Other sessions (Session 9: Relationships module; Session 4: Self-Regulation module) provide the opportunity to explore the young person's own experiences of inappropriate sexual boundaries – for example, when their own parents or carers failed to provide a safe environment for them – and consider how such inappropriate sexual behaviours or exposure has impacted on their own development. They also provide an opportunity for the adolescent to reframe these experiences and develop a positive future self-narrative in which these experiences can be accommodated.

6. Insight: Impact of HSB on victim

A common feature of many intervention programmes for sexual offenders is victim empathy work. This *Change for Good* manual includes this focus in a number of ways. First, timeline work is also used to help the young person in treatment to explicitly think about the impact of their actions on another person's future and contrast that with what their future might have looked like had they not been abused. Such forward thinking about negative consequences is likely to have been largely ignored in the immediacy of abuse, and subsequently repressed.

Second, there are several sessions focused on developing insight into the nature of the victim's experience. Two precursors are provided before this begins: the initial step is several tasks to develop the young person's ability to imagine and understand other people's point of view; and this is followed by an elaboration of the events around the HSB incident to act as an anchor for the subsequent exploration of the victim's thoughts and feelings. The adolescent is asked to consider what they imagined their victim was thinking and feeling *at the time* of the abuse, and contrast that with what they imagine *now* – after they have had a chance to reflect. This is also an opportunity to help the young person identify ways in which, at a cognitive level, they can show a series of thinking errors (e.g. misinterpretation, minimisation, jumping to conclusions) that allows them to distort the reality of the victim's experience in order to make it easier to create an internal rationale where abuse is acceptable. The hope is that creating a more tangible sense of the consequences of the abuse for the victim makes such distorted thinking more difficult in future.

7. Mentalisation ability

At all stages of the *Change for Good* programme outlined in the manual and CD-ROM the clinician should aim to develop the young person's mentalisation ability. This refers to their ability to think in a psychological way about their own thoughts, feelings and behaviour as well as those of other people. For example, in the Self-Regulation module the young person is helped to identify the thoughts triggered in themselves by certain situations in which they normally become angry – and then helped to explore how these might be related to underlying beliefs. While cognitive therapy typically aims to shift dysfunctional assumptions and beliefs (or construct more adaptive alternatives) increasing mentalisation ability relates to developing the young person's capacity to think effectively in a psychological way.

While working through the various tasks presented in this manual, it can be helpful to bear in mind the need to:

- *cultivate curiosity* in the young person to identify and explore their own thoughts and beliefs and those of others

- *model a reflective and questioning stance* where alternative accounts are considered as possible explanations of behaviour (e.g. *'It sounds like you are saying... Is that right? ...I wonder how that fits with what you said earlier? ...It occurs to me that...'*)

- *promote perspective taking:* help the young person look at things from other people's point of view, and thus understand (but perhaps not agree with) their actions (*'Put yourself in the position of your mother for a few minutes. Pretend that X has just happened/been said. So you are your mother... What are you feeling now as your mother? What are you thinking?...'*); this approach is helpful in promoting reflection about the young person's relationships with others (including you)

- *develop an understanding of feelings:* how emotions can be at times confusing, move up and down and how they can in a given moment distort our thinking

- *help reframe past experiences* in way that is balanced and realistic and which is consistent with a new and coherent narrative about themselves.

The clinician-adolescent relationship also provides an immediate framework to promote mentalisation ability in the young person. There are important moment-to-moment fluctuations in rapport (akin to the psychodynamic construct of transference) as the clinician's words, behaviour or inflections elicit conscious and unconscious responses from the young person. These should be carefully monitored because they provide an important insight into the adolescent's model of interacting with the world and an opportunity for therapeutic intervention. For example, a young person who has experienced early maltreatment may have come to react in an intuitively hostile or defensive way to relatively neutral cues from the clinician. It is important that the clinician is able to step back and take a 'meta' position in relation to these responses and maintain an ongoing commentary or set of invitations that articulate how the young person *might be feeling*. For example, the clinician might comment: *'I'm not sure but I get a sense that you may not have liked what I have just said. Things were going well, and that seems to have put you off. What do you think?'* These are explicit invitations for the young person to mentalise. As such, the moment-to-moment interactions within the therapy can act as the raw material to help the young person develop their mentalisation skills and uncover some of the vulnerabilities that may lie at the heart of their difficulties. For clinicians who are trained in psychoanalytic techniques, these issues will be extremely familiar as they relate directly to the relationship transference.

8. Understanding and managing HSB

The work in this area extends across all modules. The focus in the Relationships module is on being honest about what actually happened during the abusive incident(s) and considering the impact on the victim and on themselves – both at the time and in the future. There is also work towards the end of the module to clarify explicitly what is meant by abuse, distinguishing between healthy and unhealthy sexual behaviour. The Self-Regulation module develops these themes, helping the adolescent (as described above) identify 'signals' that can indicate risk situations and encouraging them to develop strategies for dealing with these. Of equal importance is the ongoing work to help the young person develop a narrative in which they can make sense of their past harmful sexual behaviour and see a future self that acts in positive and socially appropriate ways.

Identifying situations, thoughts and feelings associated with increased risk of HSB is a common intervention component. It follows from a cognitive behavioural model where the clinician works with the young person to help them identify:

- **situations** that may contribute to increased risk: these might be places (e.g. playgrounds) or events (e.g. an experience of rejection, viewing pornography, family disagreements, arguing, spending time alone)
- **thoughts** associated with increased risk. These can be in a number of forms:
    - Triggering thoughts: 'Nobody cares about me'; 'I'll show them'
    - Planning thoughts: 'We can start playing this game – there is nothing wrong with that'
    - Minimising thoughts: 'A little touching won't matter'
    - Excusing thoughts: 'She wants it to happen'; 'I'll stop if she doesn't like it'
    - Manipulating thoughts: 'I'll pretend it was an accident'
- **feelings** associated with increased risk. These can vary a great deal across individual children – it is important to identify which feelings appear to be relevant to each case. HSB may be associated, for example, with:
    - low mood (e.g. feeling unhappy or unloved)
    - anger (e.g. following rejection or a sense of injustice)
    - boredom
    - sexual arousal

- more distal behaviours that increase the general risk level – for example, getting into fights, arguing, spending time alone, looking at pornography.

As the young person becomes more able to identify those factors that are likely to contribute to increased risk there needs to be a complementary focus on techniques and strategies that help them avoid such situations and manage them when they arise. These strategies can be related to each level; for example:

- *Situation:* Role playing an invitation to baby-sit
- *Thoughts:* Thought stopping and distraction
- *Feelings:* Using support network
- *Behaviours:* Alternative activity plan.

9. Taking responsibility

A crucial nested task within the narrative work is engaging with the young person's account of their harmful sexual behaviour. This can feature varying levels of denial, minimisation and projection of responsibility onto external factors (either other people or events). For example, descriptions such as 'It was an accident'; 'They wanted it to happen'; 'They enjoyed it'; 'My dad knew it was going to happen'; and 'I shouldn't have been left on my own' are pretty typical descriptions. This approach must be understood at some level as a defence that the young person is using to protect themselves, at least psychically. If they say 'Yes – I was completely responsible' one needs to consider what the implications of such acceptance would be for their own constructed view of themselves. Will that mean that they are then an evil or unlovable person? While we may know that this is not true, to work successfully with a young person's denial we must understand or at least have an *hypothesised treatment formulation* as to why it is so difficult for them to accept that they are at fault. The clinician's job is to help them create a narrative that allows acceptance of responsibility but does not undermine their sense that they are a valid and valuable person.

In working with the young person's story about their HSB the clinician should help them construct a narrative:

- in which they accept responsibility for their actions
- in which they make a distinction between their actions (unacceptable) and who they are as a person (valued and important). In other words the narrative should not have global and negative implications for them as a person
- that acknowledges the impact of their actions on others, particularly their victim, but also on themselves and their future
- that articulates their intention to behave in ways that are acceptable and respectful of others in the future.

Work on responsibility takes place first in the Relationships module (Session 2) where the concept of a responsibility pie-chart is introduced and continues in the Self-Regulation module (Session 5) where the adolescent's attribution of responsibility is revisited and explored further. Acknowledging the fact that taking responsibility is likely to be a difficult process (rather than a single event) and that denial can often be an entrenched defence can make it easier for the clinician to take a patient but persistent stance on this issue. As such, helping the young person take more responsibility for their past and future actions should be seen as an ongoing and iterative task throughout the intervention.

10. Healthy vs. harmful sexual behaviour

A primary reason why the young person is being offered therapy is in order to address their problems with harmful sexual behaviour. These problems are typically associated with past experiences of abuse (sexual or otherwise) and/or exposure to lax or inappropriate sexual boundaries. This means that often the young person has:

1. inadequate or inaccurate knowledge about sexual development and behaviour
2. distorted attitudes/beliefs relating to sexual behaviour
3. distorted attitudes/beliefs relating to intimacy, relationships and consent.

The task during therapy is on the one hand to challenge and correct these erroneous views but at the same time help the young person develop a positive and appropriate view of sexuality in general, and more specifically, a positive narrative about themselves as a healthy sexual person now and in the future. In other words, it is not sufficient to correct the young person's perspective – in addition, the clinical task is to develop a positive alternative that is relevant and acceptable to the adolescent (and of course to society). These issues are covered specifically in the first two sessions of the Road Map for the Future module which also include Quizzes in relation to sex and sexuality. The focus here is likely to vary a great deal across individuals depending on their awareness of facts about sex, distorted attitudes around sexuality (especially regarding women and homosexuality) and fears or uncertainty about their own sexual orientation. The clinician is encouraged to help the young person draw a very clear distinction between what sexual behaviour is acceptable and what is not.

ADAPTING THE MANUAL

As highlighted in Chapter 1, the *Change for Good* book and CD-ROM should be seen primarily as a clinical resource. It does not contain the material required for treating every adolescent, nor will the balance of the work (for example, in relation to anger vs. sexual preoccupation with children) be appropriate for every case. The clinician is encouraged to use their treatment formulation to reflect on which of the ten main treatment areas are most relevant to the young person they are seeing in treatment and create a treatment plan consistent with these needs; there may of course be additional areas that need to be addressed (e.g. trauma focused work). Such planning may entail prioritising some areas over others, and even omitting some sessions or tasks that are of limited relevance. It may be sensible to recommend a 30-week treatment plan, which, after accounting for the 26 sessions provided, leaves four sessions free to be tailored to the particular needs of each adolescent.

Changing the ordering or sequence of sessions

Depending on the formulation it may be helpful or indeed necessary to change the sequence of sessions compared to the suggested ordering given here. For example, in cases where issues of aggression or a salient risk of sexual acting out are evident, it may be sensible to prioritise the content of the Self-Regulation module first over the Relationships module to help the young person manage their immediate behavioural problems. In other cases the work in relation to psycho-social education (the last two sessions in the Relationships module) may be postponed until the 'Road Map for the Future' module to allow work to progress more quickly to issues of self-regulation and strategies to manage problematic sexual and aggressive behaviour. In other words the material presented here should primarily be seen as a set of resources covering many of the relevant areas that should be covered in treatment. The sessions have been sequenced to provide clarity and one suggested 'route map' – however, it is imperative that the therapist considers the optimal sequence of the material in relation to the particular young person with whom they are engaging in treatment. Obviously, in order to do this successfully, it is necessary for the therapist to have adequate familiarity with all session material prior to beginning their first case.

Adapting the manual for adolescents with learning difficulties

In addition to adapting the manual on the basis of the treatment formulation, it is also important to be mindful of the strengths and limitations of the young person in engaging with therapy more generally. As noted in Chapter 2 a high proportion of young people who come to the attention of services due to sexually harmful behaviour have some form of learning disability (LD); these individuals may require an extended programme of intervention. Learning disability refers to a significant impairment in intellectual functioning (usually defined as an intelligent quotient of 70 or below) combined with significant impairments in the ability to cope adaptively and independently (Department of Health, 2001). The assessment process should therefore entail a relevant assessment of general intellectual functioning conducted by a properly trained educational or clinical psychologist.

The genesis of HSB may be exacerbated by learning difficulties but is unlikely to be caused by them. For example, poor social skills and limited positive engagement with peers and adults may potentiate some elements in pathways to sexual offending (Lindsay, 2005). In relation to the latter, there is an extensive literature documenting the barriers and stigma associated with LD in successfully engaging in occupational, leisure and social activities. These make it especially difficult for a young person to develop the expectations of a positive identity and life that are central to a non-offending trajectory.

There is some evidence that the victims of sex offenders with LD (adolescent and adult) are more likely to be male and younger than the victims of non-LD sex offenders (Blanchard *et al.*, 1999; Fortune and Lambie, 2004). In addition, recidivism appears to be higher for learning disabled perpetrators (Craig and Hutchinson, 2005). The actual dynamics and proximal factors of the sexual offending in this population appear to be remarkably similar to non-learning disabled individuals. The following general factors are common features:

- grooming behaviour (Parry and Lindsay, 2003)
- anti-social attitudes (Lindsay, Elliott and Astell, 2004)
- denial and minimisation (Sefarbi, 1990).

Individuals with learning disability often display some or all of the following difficulties:

- slow speed of processing information
- memory and learning deficits (for example, reduced short-term memory)
- limited understanding of abstract information (i.e. a concrete thinking style limiting the understanding of metaphor)
- difficulties in language understanding and expression
- limited knowledge of everyday rules, social norms, and commonly known facts
- attentional problems (i.e. difficulties in concentrating for sustained periods)
- limited ability to evaluate knowledge and form independent opinions (i.e. can be compliant and/or suggestible).

Depending on the precise difficulties that a learning disabled young person presents with, the following revisions to therapy may be useful:

- increase the number of sessions accordingly
- spread the content of some sessions over a longer period
- reduce the duration of an individual session
- increase the number of sessions per week
- repeat key points a number of times within and across sessions
- reduce the amount of new information given in any one session
- limit the use of metaphor (these can be difficult to understand for individuals with concrete thinking styles)
- use more examples, with pictures to illustrate if possible

- present concepts using a variety of sensory modalities – for example: word, picture, gesture, simple symbols, objects and toys (especially when these concepts are complex, such as emotions and thoughts).

Specific adaptations can be made to the clinical techniques used in the manual. For example, when using the visual timeline it can be helpful to capture the young person's experiences, thoughts and feelings in a visual way rather than with words. Cut-out images from magazines and newspapers, symbols (e.g. smiling and frowning faces), drawings of events, stick people and key objects are all possible options. Furthermore, colour can be used in a meaningful way: red to mark offending behaviour, thoughts or feelings while green can be used to mark more adaptive or pro-social responses. Risky thoughts such as those minimising responsibility, danger or harm can be personalised into people such as Mr Ignorant, Mr Sneaky and Mr Nasty (respectively). Similarly, helpful thoughts such as those that take responsibility, consider the harm to the victim and spot danger can be personalised into people such as Mr Honest, Mr Kind and Mr Think Twice (Ayland and West, 2006). Here, the age of the young person, as well as their level of cognitive ability, need to be considered in gauging whether the adolescent will find the approach patronising.

The character library can serve as an important resource to help a young person identify feelings in themselves or others. The clinician can ask them to choose which facial expression fits from a set of expressions for a given character rather than asking the young person to name a feeling. Once they have chosen an expression the clinician can suggest and explore different names for it.

More generally, the clinician should use language that is simple and clear. Conclusions should be simplified to two or three point messages at most. An example of this is given in Session 3 in the Relationships module where a simple three tick definition is provided for sexual abuse:

Sex is okay if:

☑ The person is over 16

☑ The person is happy and free to choose

☑ The person clearly says 'yes they want to have sex'.

If the three boxes aren't ticked then it is abuse.

Given the difficulties often experienced in the social domain in individuals with learning difficulties, the clinician may judge it important to spend relatively more time developing skills in this area. Promoting greater positive engagement may be facilitated by:

- spending more time exploring with the young person the nature of their social life, at home and at school

- identifying with the young person how they might like their social life to be different, the reasons why it isn't like this, and the ways any obstacles might be overcome. (The clinician might decide to include a number of problem-solving sessions to address these obstacles. These should help the young person identify the strengths they have already and use role-play to build confidence and provide explicit learning experiences. Realistic goals should also be set for the young person between sessions (for example, telephoning a friend).)

MEASURING CHANGE

A number of assessment measures should have been administered during the adolescent's initial clinical assessment alongside a clinical evaluation of risk. These can form the basis for any reassessment following the termination of treatment.

There are a range of measures that can be used to measure change during treatment for HSB; however, a standardised battery with norms is not available in the same way as for work with mainstream child and adolescent disorders such as depression and anxiety. As such, it may be necessary to tailor-make a battery of evaluation measures, some of which are quite generic in nature and others which are more associated with specific aspects of behaviour or disturbance that are known to be associated with HSB. Below we provide some examples of measures that span sexual behaviour, attitudes and psychological functioning.

The Strengths and Difficulties Questionnaire (SDQ; Goodman, 1997)

This short questionnaire is a widely used and respected behavioural screening measure designed to be used with children and adolescents aged between 3 and 16 years of age. It enquires about 25 attributes, some positive and others problematic, which combine to form five scales. These include: emotional symptoms; conduct problems; hyperactivity/inattention; peer relationship problems; and pro-social behaviour. There are parent, teacher and self-report versions. A full description and the scales are freely available at www.sdqinfo.org.

Trauma Symptom Checklist for Children (TSCC; Briere, 1996)

This is a self-report measure of post-traumatic distress and related psychological symptomatology particularly sensitive to experiences of sexual abuse. The questionnaire comprises 54 items and takes between 10 and 20 minutes to complete. It is validated for use with children aged 8–16 years old. It measures post-traumatic difficulties along six scales: anxiety, depression, anger, post-traumatic stress, dissociation and sexual concerns (including subscales of sexual preoccupation and sexual distress). It also contains two validity scales checking that the respondent has not potentially under- or over-reported symptoms. The scale can be obtained from: Psychological Assessment Resources, Box 998, Odessa, FL 33556; 1-800-331-TEST. Website: www.parinc.com.

Rosenberg Self-Esteem Scale (Rosenberg, 1965)

This is the most established measure of global, explicit self-esteem. It has been validated within a wide range of child and adult age groups. Participants are asked to rate their level of agreement for ten statements describing themselves using a 4-point scale. The measure is easily accessible from the web (e.g. www.yorku.ca/rokada/psyctest/rosenbrg.pdf).

Adolescent Sexual Behavior Inventory (ASBI); Parent and Self-Report (Friedrich et al., 2004)

These two measures provide an index of both positive and negative sexual behaviours. Both scales are based around five similar factors relating to: sexual knowledge/interest; deviant sexual interests; sexual risk/misuse; sexual fear; and concerns about appearance. There are 50 items altogether and the measure takes around 10 or 12 minutes to complete.

Child Behavior Checklist (CBCL; Achenbach and Edelbrock, 1991); Youth Self-Report (Achenbach, 1991)

These are excellent comprehensive measures that capture wider mental health and behaviour problems (e.g. anxiety, depression, conduct problems, attentional problems). They are well validated and are accompanied by normative data. Website: www.aseba.org.

The NCATS Assessment Questionnaire (McCrory, 2007 unpublished)

This is a short screening questionnaire developed in the context of a fourth tier clinical service to provide a basic assessment of the adolescent's view of their HSB. It allows the clinician to cover a range of issues related to a specific harmful sexual incident in a relatively unthreatening manner. The questions cover: responsibility (1, 2 and 7); remorse (4, 6); sexual pleasure (3, 9); empathy (5, 8); social isolation (12, 15); mood (11, 13); and coping strategies (10, 14). It is short (only 15 items) and simple to administer but has not yet been validated or normed. Within the NCATS clinical service, however, it has been shown to be sensitive to change pre- and post-treatment. A copy of this questionnaire is included below.

NCATS Questionnaire

Please rate the following statements as honestly as possible. When answering each question you need to think about the sexual incident with another young person.

Each answer is scored from 1–5. Please choose the number that best reflects your view.

    1 = Strongly disagree

    2 = Disagree

    3 = Neither agree nor disagree

    4 = Agree

    5 = Strongly agree

1. I was completely responsible for what happened sexually.
   Strongly disagree   ①---------②---------③---------④---------⑤   Strongly agree

2. The other person was responsible for what happened.
   Strongly disagree   ①---------②---------③---------④---------⑤   Strongly agree

3. I got some enjoyment from what happened.
   Strongly disagree   ①---------②---------③---------④---------⑤   Strongly agree

4. In reality the incident was no big deal.
   Strongly disagree   ①---------②---------③---------④---------⑤   Strongly agree

5. Deep down the other young person wanted something sexual to happen.
   Strongly disagree   ①---------②---------③---------④---------⑤   Strongly agree

6. I feel guilty thinking about what I did.
   Strongly disagree   ①---------②---------③---------④---------⑤   Strongly agree

7. It wasn't my fault.
   Strongly disagree   ①---------②---------③---------④---------⑤   Strongly agree

8. I really understand how the other young person must have felt.
   Strongly disagree   ①---------②---------③---------④---------⑤   Strongly agree

9. I sometimes become sexually excited thinking about what happened.
   Strongly disagree   ①---------②---------③---------④---------⑤   Strongly agree

10. I am able to talk easily to other people about my problems.

Strongly disagree   ①--------②---------③---------④---------⑤   Strongly agree

11. I often feel low and depressed.

Strongly disagree   ①--------②---------③---------④---------⑤   Strongly agree

12. I find it difficult to make friends.

Strongly disagree   ①--------②---------③---------④---------⑤   Strongly agree

13. I feel very positive about my future.

Strongly disagree   ①--------②---------③---------④---------⑤   Strongly agree

14. I have lots of ways of dealing with my sexual worries.

Strongly disagree   ①--------②---------③---------④---------⑤   Strongly agree

15. I spend a lot of time by myself.

Strongly disagree   ①--------②---------③---------④---------⑤   Strongly agree

SOME THOUGHTS ON CONCURRENT WORK WITH PARENTS AND CARERS

A comprehensive guide to concurrent work with parents is beyond the scope of this manual, the remit of which is the individual work with the adolescent. Nevertheless, it is important to acknowledge the importance of concurrent systemic work, which we recommend takes place in parallel with any individual intervention programme. The frequency of such work, and the roles of the people involved (parents, carers, key workers, social workers), will vary. Here we outline some general principles relevant to working with carers and parents in particular.

First, it is necessary to clarify the nature of any work with parents. The contract with the parent is that sessions are there in order to support the young person in treatment. In other words the focus of the sessions is on the adolescent and their needs, rather than on the needs of the parents. However, as we discuss below, such a distinction in practice is rarely clear. Partnership is based on the premise of collaboration where the parents should be invited to join with the clinician in thinking about the problems presented by the adolescent in their care as well as how they as parents are responding to these problems. It should be highlighted from the outset that this partnership takes place in the context of open confidentiality such that the parents are in agreement that the work must adhere to child protection procedures. This agreement should be laid out at the beginning of the young person's treatment and should be non-negotiable.

Second, parental sessions should ideally be offered by a different clinician to the one delivering the intervention to the young person. Conflicts regarding confidentiality and treatment alliance (or in psychoanalytic terms, split transference) are likely to arise if a single clinician is working across both strands. However, it is helpful to have the treating clinician present at any review meetings together with the parents, the parental clinician, and the adolescent in treatment.

Third, the content of the work with parents should include some general description of the work that the adolescent is completing as part of the intervention. This will familiarise the parents with the main themes and issues that are being covered. Note that this is not the same as reporting the actual clinical material from the individual sessions with the adolescent (which is often of a very personal nature); this should remain confidential. Clinical judgement may be required when it appears important to broach a relevant issue that has been raised by the young person. On these occasions, it can be helpful to seek the adolescent's permission to raise the matter with the parents; however, such a consideration should be over-ridden if the matter reflects a child protection concern, with the young person themselves or another person being placed at risk. The work with parents should also be practical and supportive, helping them deal with the often challenging experience of negotiating with the young person's school and managing relationships with other professionals.

Fourth, the powerful feelings that harmful sexual behaviour can elicit, in parents or in foster carers, cannot be under-estimated. Such behaviour can be associated with profound feelings of shame, guilt, anger, bewilderment, sadness and even humiliation. While the nature of such feelings will vary across cases, the traumatic impact of abuse perpetrated by a child within a family can serve to undermine a parent's sense of competence and at the same time destabilise the family system. The parents (or their previous partners) may have been partly responsible for failing to provide adequate care and boundaries for the adolescent leading to uncomfortable feelings of guilt. The consequence is that relationships are typically disrupted, with a loss of trust accompanied by feelings of stress and disorientation. Parents have a conflictual set of feelings about their child which can overwhelm them at a time when they are already feeling deskilled and incompetent. Deep feelings of shame can also cut parents off from normal sources of support and help, as other family members and friends are avoided. Parental work should be an opportunity for parents to process the strong feelings elicited by their child's harmful sexual behaviour and a chance to help increase confidence in their ability to provide good parenting – by supporting their child in therapy and at the same time providing boundaries at home that are consistent and balanced. The parents' own history, attitudes towards sex and sexuality, and in particular experiences of previous traumas or abuse are likely to impact on this process.

Fifth, the sexualised behaviour shown by the adolescent needs to be discussed in an open and clear way. Fathers in particular can find such material difficult to broach; however, avoidance is unlikely to help the adolescent develop a sense of containment and understanding about what is acceptable and what is not. Parents and carers need to be helped to think about implementing appropriate boundaries and consider the obstacles (both within themselves and in relation to the adolescent) that might make this difficult. Sometimes basic issues of risk (e.g. access to the internet) can be simply addressed. At the same time, parents should be helped to remain emotionally accessible to the adolescent when they are withdrawn or depressed and are seeking support.

The scholarly work of Arnon Bentovim is particularly recommended for those who wish to consider further the clinical issues and challenges related to working with families in the context of disclosed abuse; see Bentovim (1995 and 2004).

Chapter 5

Module Descriptions

MODULE 1: ENGAGEMENT – PREPARING THE YOUNG PERSON FOR CHANGE

Engaging with adolescents who present with HSB can be a challenging task. Yet the potential for later therapeutic change in large measure depends on getting this initial stage of the intervention right. For this reason we have included a discrete module on engagement that provides a structure around which a sound therapeutic relationship can be established. The objectives of the engagement module are several-fold and include:

- establishing a good rapport and therapeutic alliance
- developing a better understanding of the young person in order to inform a clearer formulation of their problem
- helping the young person acknowledge that there is a problem that can be helped
- eliciting motivation for change by developing a discrepancy between where the young person is now and where they would like to be.

Why can engagement be such a tricky process? Usually, adolescents coming to treatment for HSB will not have referred themselves – they are likely to have been referred by others, or even mandated to attend by a court. As a result they may begin with little or no sense of ownership over the process. Often they do not think they need 'treatment' or 'therapy'. If they do not deny outright their HSB (not uncommon) then they usually minimise their behaviour, describing it as something which occurred in the past, that was not that serious in the first place, or which was someone else's fault. This means that starting with HSB as the primary focus of the work may potentially create a setting for conflict and non-compliance. Young people may be reluctant, angry, anxious, withdrawn or uninterested. The strategy we outline here is designed to work with young people who may present with ambivalence or antipathy.

Instead of beginning with a focus on a 'problem' we suggest using a visual timeline as a central tool for engagement. This is a concrete space that is elaborated in different ways across each session, with different details being added about the young person's past experience as well as future aspirations. Using a timeline as the central plank of the engagement process has a number of distinct advantages.

1. Adolescents can be particularly self-conscious. Sitting alone with a clinician in a room can feel potentially persecuting and threatening. Using a visual timeline provides a neutral external focus that both the clinician and young person can work with in establishing a therapeutic alliance.

2. The young person is likely to have a number of anxieties and fears about coming for treatment which in turn serve to fuel their minimisation and denial. Part of this derives from a tendency to think of their HSB as a defining aspect of who they are as a person (that they are 'evil', 'bad', 'unlovable' etc). The prospect of therapy can then loom large as it can seem to challenge their very sense of self. An initial focus on the young person as a whole person helps make a shift here because implicit in the timeline is the idea that the young person is a multifaceted individual with many other experiences relevant to their sense of themselves.

3. In a similar way, the timeline opens up the future as a space where the YP can begin to develop a new concept of themselves. This fits with one of the key developmental goals of adolescence – creating a new sense of self as a young adult. The advantage in terms of engagement is that a focus on the future provides leverage to create a discrepancy between where the young person is *now* and where they would *like to be* in the future.

4. Finally the timeline can act as the visual narrative helping the young person to develop a more coherent as well as a more contained view of their past experience. As has been noted, many young people presenting with HSB have had disruptive and dislocated upbringings and frequent experiences of maltreatment and poor attachment. A goal of the therapy is to help them develop a narrative where they can acknowledge responsibility for their HSB but at the same time create a positive sense of themselves and their future.

Much of the work relating to fostering change derives from the drug and alcohol field, notably the Stages of Change model (Prochaska and DiClemente, 1992) and 'motivational interviewing' (MI; Miller and Rollnick, 2002), which are described in greater detail below.

The Stages of Change model

The Stages of Change model identifies a number of stages which characterise a 'change cycle'; each young person may be at a different point in that cycle when they begin therapy.

Pre-contemplation

The pre-contemplation stage describes the first stage in the change process where the young person may not themselves see any need for change. They may be in denial that a problem exists and be angry or defensive. 'There is no need for me to be here'; 'I don't have a problem'. It is important that during the engagement process you *do not* begin by trying to persuade or convince the young person and thereby precipitate argument or withdrawal; such an approach will almost certainly fail to elicit change. Rather, your aim is to elicit from the young person their thoughts and views on change. This is achieved by means of the timeline by helping the young person consider where they are now, and reflect on how they would like things to be different. In essence, this is creating discrepancy between where the young person is now and where they would like to be. At the same time there is a need to be clear why the young person is in treatment; in the first session there is a need to articulate clearly these reasons and your understanding about their HSB.

Contemplation

The next stage relates to contemplation which moves thinking about change forward to explore any ambivalence or difficulties that may stand in the way of change. Here, it is important to first acknowledge the uncertainties that the young person may present with, then, in addition, help them to consider ways in which change can be achieved. In this module, looking at developing skills and values is a very concrete way to conceptualise how change might be initiated.

Subsequent stages

Subsequent stages of change – preparation and action – represent the primary content of future sessions, as does the maintenance of change and the avoidance of relapse.

Developing rapport

The importance of establishing a good therapeutic alliance is a central element in maximising the likelihood of a good outcome; this has already been highlighted in Chapter 4. Many young people begin therapy with a mixture of anxiety, resentment and ambivalence: these feelings pose real challenges for even the most experienced clinician. Maintaining an awareness of how the young person is responding to the material can represent a powerful intervention in itself. The following dialogue illustrates the point:

> T: *Tell me about your family.*
>
> YP: *There is just me, my brother and my mum.*
>
> T: *Anyone else? What about your dad?*
>
> YP: *No… Why are you asking all this? You know about my family already.*
>
> T: *So there is your mum and your brother. Let's put them up on the board.*
>
> YP: *(Crosses his arms and looks away.)*
>
> T: *Thanks John – that's helpful. I noticed though when I asked about your dad you didn't look too happy. I wonder if you'd rather I didn't ask you about your dad at the moment. Is that right?*
>
> YP: *(Nods.)*
>
> T: *Thanks. I know these things can be difficult. Perhaps we can come back to thinking about your dad later on. But for now, tell me about your brother. What kind of things do you both like to do together?*

Here the clinician is maintaining awareness of the moment-to-moment interaction and in particular the emotional responses of the young person reflected in their verbal and non-verbal behaviour. These responses are acknowledged in a way that helps the young person mentalise – and create a verbal representation of how they are feeling. In addition, however (and here the process departs from strictly psychoanalytic approaches), the nature of the young person's response is used to explicitly shape how the collaborative task of therapy is pursued. At times the responses of the young person may be incorporated into the task in a way that helps them to represent their feelings in an explicit way.

Most adolescents presenting with HSB have also experienced some form of abuse or early adversity (for example, exposure to domestic violence). The clinician should feel able to genuinely empathise (either tacitly or explicitly) with these early maltreatment experiences across the intervention; it is only fair that a failure by other adults to appropriately care for and protect a young person is acknowledged. This is an important part of building a rapport. The challenge, however, is to be able to express this empathy as part of a broader therapeutic approach within which the adolescent's experiences as a victim *and* their harmful sexual behaviour as a perpetrator are addressed. It would be wrong in other words for a clinician to fail to be empathic and concerned for the young person, but equally it would be wrong for them to overly identify with the young person's victim role and fail to address issues of sexual harm and the need to take responsibility. Striking the right balance here goes to the heart of a successful intervention with this client group.

The techniques and principles of motivational interviewing

As you begin work with the young person it is important to ensure that you strike a relaxed but confident tone. It can be helpful to communicate to the young person that you are experienced in working with other young people who have shown harmful sexual behaviour and that you are unlikely to be surprised by any of the issues they may raise.

A key principle of the motivational interviewing approach is that motivation is *elicited* not by being directive but by generating material from the client that allows a discrepancy to be created. The use of straightforward and open-ended questions is critical here. Avoiding direct persuasion isn't the same thing as condoning inappropriate or illegal behaviours. The job of the clinician is to acknowledge ambivalence that the young person might express and help them go through a process where they weigh up the pros and cons of change. Inappropriate views are acknowledged – *'It sounds like you think it is not a serious thing to touch a child sexually'* – but also challenged: *'If your social worker was here, what would they say? What would your mother say? ...So it sounds like there are different views about this. Later in the programme we will think together about why touching a child sexually – is a serious problem.'*

A young person's willingness to change will vary across time, and during some sessions they will be more receptive than others. Experiences outside the session and changes of mood can alter the level of openness to change and the level of engagement; these fluctuations should be expected and not taken personally. Work with these fluctuations and be open to explore and acknowledge expressions of ambivalence (verbal or non-verbal). Remember that facilitating the articulation of ambivalence is an important goal in its own right.

There are a range of techniques associated with motivational interviewing. If you wish to learn more about these then refer to the latest edition of the motivational interviewing handbook (Miller and Rollnick, 2002). General therapeutic techniques include:

- asking open questions
- listening reflectively
- affirming or providing positive feedback where appropriate
- summarising.

A specific strategy in motivational interviewing relates to eliciting 'change talk'. At a practical level, the young person is encouraged to reflect on their current and past situation and consider the disadvantages of the status quo. They are then encouraged to consider the advantages of change and develop optimism that such change is possible. Developing the discrepancy between current and past behaviours and future goals acts then as one catalyst for change during subsequent sessions.

Overview of sessions

Session 1: Making an Authentic Connection

There is a great deal of material in this first session. It is important not to rush it and try to complete all the elements. The information-giving part can be naturally spread over future sessions if necessary. The most important element is that you remain containing and reflective and ensure that the reason why the young person is here is explored and acknowledged. It is also important to help the young person articulate how they wish to change, and in particular how their life might be different at the end of the therapeutic process. This session and accompanying home project as they appear in full in the CD-ROM is included in the samples section at the back of this book.

Session 2: Looking to the Future I

Some more information about the nature of therapy is provided – in particular the nature of the session structure. Modelling setting an agenda with the young person is an important demonstration of the collaborative nature of the therapeutic relationship (see Chapter 4, The Delivery of a Typical Session p.51). The task is to present how future sessions will be structured, and then elaborate the young person's goals and aspirations for the future in relation to their job or college plans, their social life and other interests. These are used to elaborate the future part of the timeline. Developing a clear picture in each of these areas is an important task as this material is often referred back to in subsequent sessions. Some time is given in the latter part of the session to thinking about the impact of another episode of HSB on their likelihood of meeting their future goals.

Session 3: Looking to the Future II

This session shifts the focus back to the young person's earlier development and provides a space to identify key aspects of their lives. Again, they are invited to put these on the timeline along with positive experiences and achievements as well as relationships. The skills or attributes used by the young person at these points are drawn out by the clinician who, at the end of the session, summarises three areas important for reaching their goals: 'being in the driving seat' (self-regulation); relationship skills; and general problem solving. The young person – the absence of absolute denial permitting – may be able to consider what would have helped them avoid their harmful sexual behaviour.

Session 4 (Optional): What I Believe In (optional)

This session introduces the character library and includes two fictional vignettes that introduce the idea of values. The clinician may judge that it is not necessary to extend the engagement process by including this session and prioritise moving on to the next module. The vignettes are designed to elicit from the young person thoughts on what constitute important values that guide behaviour. They are asked to prepare key scenes in the vignettes by laminating the figures and backgrounds provided on the CD-ROM. In discussion with the young person, the clinician should draw out five core values and consider how these values (and their absence) are related to future success and happiness, as well as to harmful sexual behaviour.

MODULE 2: RELATIONSHIPS – CULTIVATING ADAPTIVE RELATIONSHIP SKILLS

This module focuses on the interpersonal aspects of the adolescent's life – their attachments and relationships to others. This encompasses family members, friends, teachers and in particular those who have been victim to their harmful sexual behaviour.

As we considered briefly in Chapter 2, the adolescent stage of development is characterised by a shift from a primary affiliation with family to a greater identification with peers. The perceptions, values and respect of peers begins to acquire a new level of importance. This heightened sensitivity to evaluation comes at a time when puberty drives the development of a new social and sexual identity, which can elicit confusion, excitement, anxiety and self-consciousness. It is hardly surprising that for many young people adolescence poses real challenges, particularly in the social domain. There is a need for them to reconfigure previously established 'child–adult' relationships that no longer fit with their increasingly adult bodies and to develop knowledge and competence in relation to romantic and sexual relationships.

For young people with harmful sexual behaviour meeting these generic challenges can be particularly difficult. As has already been noted on several occasions, many children have had previous maltreatment experiences that have compromised their ability to develop age appropriate relationships; these experiences have tended to reduce their ability to regulate their behaviour and emotions and at the same time have shaped maladaptive beliefs and expectations about others accompanied by patterns of poor attachment. While the child's developing sexuality is distinct from the nature of their attachment these two factors are inevitably related. Caregivers who harm or neglect their children can, by their actions, establish and reinforce maladaptive and even deviant patterns of sexual response and behaviour.

The role of attachment as a framework within which to understand young people with harmful sexual behaviour has become increasingly influential (see Rich, 2006). Defining precisely what is meant by attachment during adolescence remains problematic; nonetheless, several aspects of attachment theory represent a useful 'rule of thumb' for thinking about their relationship problems. Exploring the adolescent's deficits in attachment and their internal working model of relationships can help provide the clinician with a way of linking the young person's victimisation and prior adverse experiences with their current sexual aggression. A wide range of clinical and research approaches have been used to categorise and model child attachment. For the purposes of this intervention it is helpful for the clinician to think about attachment at two levels.

First, one should consider the adolescent's attachment to their parents. A young person presenting with HSB may not have had an experience of a dependable reliable parent who was capable of helping them develop a sense of security and emotional safety and who promoted social competence and mentalisation skills. Exploring the thoughts, feelings and behaviours that adolescents hold towards their parents and caregivers can shed light on their model of relationships towards others. It also provides an opportunity for the clinician to help the young person create a more coherent and integrated narrative about their relationships and past experiences of victimisation that can help them as they endeavour to create a new self-identity.

Second, the clinician can think about relevant attachment dimensions. These can be thought about in many different ways. For our purposes the following four dimensions can be a helpful framework to use for each individual case.

1. Self-representations
    - Agency: Sense of self as a person capable of acting on the world
    - Self-efficacy: Confidence in effectively accomplishing goals
    - Connectedness: View of relationship with parents and the wider social group

2. Attachment behaviours
    - Proximity-seeking: Behaviours bringing self in to contact with others
    - Expressive behaviours: Communicating own feelings and wishes to others
    - Reciprocity: Behaviours responding to the feelings and wishes of others
    - Exploration: Behaviours that enable safe exploration of the physical and emotional environment

3. Attachment capacities
    - Empathy: Ability to experience understanding and concern for others
    - Mentalization: Ability to identify and understand thoughts and feelings of self/others
    - Self-regulation: Ability to regulate own feelings and behaviours in response to others

4. Attachment experience
    - Drive: Desire and interest in forming relationships
    - Satisfaction: Satisfaction and value derived from relationships with others
    - Security: Sense that relationships will provide safety, protection and wellbeing while allowing for change and flexibility

Each of these dimensions is relevant when thinking about the young person's developmental history and current presentation. Problems in one or more of these areas are likely to be relevant to their harmful sexual behaviour *and* to their overall emotional wellbeing and development. As such each session in the module focuses on one or more aspect of these attachment dimensions both in relation to the sexually abusive relationship in which the young person acted as a perpetrator but also in relation to their relationships more generally.

The goal of treatment is not a global transformation in the young person's model of relationships, but rather a realignment that moves them in the direction of more adaptive and stable relationships. The hope is that over time this shift will have cumulative and iterative benefits. In other words, a small change in relationship competence and sociability should reap reinforcing benefits well after the intervention has ceased.

Below we introduce the focus of each session. It is evident that the model used draws heavily from a CBT approach by using a collaborative, problem solving and exploratory approach. Although not explicitly a tool in the intervention, the clinician should actively formulate the young person's possible core beliefs relating to themselves (e.g. being unlovable, worthless, inadequate or a failure) and others (e.g. being unreliable, dangerous, unpredictable, exploitative etc) as part of an ongoing clinical formulation (see Chapter 4). These beliefs will invariably link to early maladaptive attachment experiences. Understanding these experiences can help the clinician formulate more accurately the young person's internal world and consider how best to pitch each session in order to engage them. The goal is to help nurture more constructive beliefs and schemas (for example, by looking at past successes and rewarding relationships).

Overview of sessions

Session 1: My Relationships

This should elicit information about the young person's relationship network and provide a basis to explore their connectedness to others. Such information will help the clinician develop a picture of their social world that will set the tone for future sessions. The young person should finish this session with an increased motivation to develop positive relationships (in order for them to meet their future goals) and an increased capacity to reflect objectively on the strengths and weaknesses of their current relationships.

Session 2: Taking Responsibility

At this point the young person's HSB is introduced. Given that the incident(s) in which the young person abused others will be a core element of the work in this and future sessions time is spent developing a 'mini-timeline' that delineates the context, actions and thoughts and feelings they had at the time as well as the victim's responses. This does not need to be completed at this stage. Rather, the core elements are sketched and the timeline remains on the wall and should be added to as new details emerge over the course of treatment. The focus during this task is not on therapeutic change per se, but working to support the adolescent to construct an accurate and as full an account of their HSB as possible in order to provide the material for future work.

The session then shifts to look at the issue of who was responsible for what happened. Here a classic CBT technique – the pie-chart – is used to visually capture the young person's views on responsibility. Then two strategies are used to encourage the young person to take more responsibility, first by working on their beliefs about what taking responsibility *means for them*, and second by questioning the allocation of responsibility to other people (or external events).

A copy of this session in full and the accompanying home project as they appear on the CD-ROM is included in the samples section at the back of this book.

Session 3: What is Sexual Abuse?

The session opens on a positive note relating to the achievements that the young person is proud of in their past. This home project from the previous session is designed to ensure they are helped to acknowledge their good qualities as well as their problem behaviour. The main task of the session then focuses on defining sexual abuse. A set of vignettes are provided to develop and consolidate their understanding. The young person is asked to evaluate which of a series of fictional incidents are abusive.

Session 4: Points of View I

The concept of perspective taking is introduced with a fictional vignette. The aim of the task is to develop empathy and mentalisation ability. A cognitive behavioural approach is used in order to help the young person identify possible thoughts and feelings each character might have given their different perspectives. These insights are then used to inform a different set of choices that the teenage boy – Jack – might make when dealing with the situation. In other words, the aim is to work on improving their self-regulation ability. A simple set of guidelines is suggested for dealing with disagreements – these include recognising and acknowledging another person's point of view.

Session 5: Points of View II

The particular focus here is in relation to the young person's own experience. They are asked to reflect on a disagreement they have had with someone else and helped to map out the sequence of events, thoughts and feelings, which occurred prior to and during the incident. They are also asked to rate how well they thought they handled the situation. A role-play task is used to encourage a greater understanding of the experience for the other person and to help them develop a new and alternative response. A model for dealing with disagreements is explicitly practised.

Session 6: Understanding My Victim's Point of View

The first part of this session adopts a perspective-taking approach similar to that taken in Session 5. The young person is invited to explore: 1. how, at the time of the abuse, they thought their victim was thinking and feeling, and 2. now that they are thinking more clearly, what they believe their victim was *really* thinking and feeling. This is as much about working with cognitive distortions as it is about developing mentalisation capacity; such distortions are common (e.g. 'They want this to happen'; 'It's only a game') and are used to underpin a false representation of what their victim felt and thought. The second part of the session is about helping the adolescent to step back and consider what factors (including cognitive distortions and sexual arousal) made it difficult for them to think clearly and regulate their behaviour appropriately at the time of their HSB.

Session 7: Consequences

The consequences of the young person's HSB – for themselves as well as for their victim – are the focus of this session. This should help construct a more realistic model of relationships and the impact that one individual can have on another. Considering the consequences for the young person of a new episode of HSB can appeal to their own self-interest; looking at the negative consequences for the victim will be helpful to some but not all young people, depending on their capacity for empathy. The homework task in this session draws on a generic sex offender treatment component – putting themselves in the position of their victim using a diary entry; the aim here is to increase empathy and reciprocity. A second task is to write a letter to their victim to increase their sense of responsibility and improve communication by articulating feelings of regret.

Session 8: Boundaries

In order to provide a framework for behavioural regulation – or appropriate behaviours in a relationship – the concepts of physical, emotional and social boundaries are introduced. How aggression in particular can break these boundaries is the focus of the latter half of the session. The young person is asked to consider experiences from their own past; this can help shed light on their internal working model of relationships and how they have internalised the expectancies of their own and others' behaviour. The session concludes by considering the impact and disadvantages of aggression.

Session 9: Sexual Boundaries

In this session a focus on boundaries extends specifically to appropriate sexual boundaries. The young person's own experience of such boundaries at home represents another important element in accurately formulating their abusive behaviour. However, it also helps the young person make sense of (but not excuse) their own HSB by considering the impact that inadequate sexual boundaries can have for children. A questionnaire from the previous session's home project then provides a means to explore what other factors may have led them to sexually harm. These factors reflect deficits in the young person's attachment capacity: 'closeness' reflects a maladaptive attempt to feel connected; 'sexual arousal' reflects maladaptive proximity seeking and drive; 'emotional arousal' reflects poor self-regulation; while 'coping strategy' could be seen as the young person's attempt to improve their sense of agency and self-efficacy.

MODULE 3: SELF-REGULATION – 'IN THE DRIVING SEAT'

This module focuses on the internal aspects of the adolescent's life – their thoughts, feelings and beliefs. One key aim is to help the young person develop their capacity to identify their feelings more accurately and to regulate their emotions more adaptively.

Adolescence and emotional regulation: From neuroscience to intervention

In Chapter 2 we discussed how adolescence is a time of marked change in the way the brain processes and regulates emotional responses. It is a time of particular malleability as there is a reorganisation of several regions of the frontal lobes implicated in emotional regulation. We know that poor self-regulation is a characteristic of conduct disorder in general (Riggs *et al.*, 2006) including young people presenting with sexually harmful behaviour.

Neuroscientific studies have begun a systematic investigation of those elements which comprise self-regulation (e.g. appraisal, planning, response selection, inhibition and monitoring). These have been variously associated with different brain regions including the dorsal and ventral regions of the anterior cingulate cortex, dorsolateral prefrontal cortex and medial and orbital frontal cortices in the frontal lobes (see Ochsner and Gross, 2005 for a review). On the other hand sub-cortical limbic regions – including the amygdala – can be viewed as the locus of the initial emotional response which in turn is regulated by these frontal systems. There is some evidence that during adolescence emotional responses are heightened compared to those of adults at a time when the regulatory systems of the frontal lobes have yet to mature. From a clinical perspective a natural goal would be first to boost regulatory competence by helping young people more effectively manage their emotional responses, and second to help moderate the intensity of emotional responses in the first place.

This module aims to promote the adolescent's ability to reflect, plan and inhibit their behaviour by developing their mentalisation ability. This can be seen as a 'top-down' intervention designed to increase the capacity of a behaviour and emotion regulatory system sub-served by the prefrontal and anterior cingulate cortices. In addition, however, this module incorporates both narrative elements and CBT techniques to help tackle maladaptive core beliefs, increase self-esteem and develop a more integrated adaptive narrative about themselves, which includes a conceptualisation of their sexually harmful behaviour. In other words there are a number of tasks that explicitly address meaning and appraisal rather than regulatory competence per se. These techniques can be thought of as a set of 'bottom-up' processes which help to modulate the young person's *reactivity* to emotional stimuli likely to be associated with changes in sub-cortical structures and the insula.

Adolescents presenting with sexually harmful behaviour are not always good at discriminating (or indeed naming) different kinds of emotions. The initial sessions focus on providing the young person with a vocabulary and framework whereby they can begin to label more accurately feelings that they have, building on the work from the Relationships module. They are also encouraged to think in a new way about the function of feelings and their communicative value. This helps foster their ability to step back and recognise their own emotional responses rather than allowing them to simply trigger impulsive behavioural reactions, including aggression.

In later sessions the young person is introduced to the link between thoughts and feelings – a core element of CBT. This helps them see that thoughts (or appraisal) in a given situation can amplify emotions or help moderate them. There is then a particular focus on the feeling of anger and aggressive responses. Not all adolescents with HSB have marked anger problems – but many do. This component should therefore be weighted more or less depending on the needs of the young person in therapy. There is a dual aim of helping them modulate their anger response (through improved mentalisation) but also providing a concrete set of behavioural and mental strategies that serve to increase their response repertoire; these can be seen as addressing both 'bottom-up' emotional reactivity and 'top-down' regulatory competence. It is important to emphasise the fact that the intervention is not about eliminating anger; rather its focus is on helping the young person respond to their feelings of anger in more adaptive ways. They are encouraged to reflect on the impact of aggressive responses in the short and longer term in order to increase their motivation to find other responses that serve their own interests as well as those of other people. This can be particularly challenging, however, given the number of young people who have observed aggressive and violent behaviours in others being rewarded materially or emotionally.

Dealing with sexual responses and feeling during sessions

It is important to continue to explore with the young person the nature of their sexual responses (to younger children for example) and provide a context where they consider the acceptability of acting on those responses either through fantasy or through their behaviour. In this context guidelines regarding what is acceptable by society and by the law must be made clear. Many adolescents remain confused as to the nature of their sexual attraction, and their sexual feelings towards others can become clearer during the progress of therapy. It is important not to see the intervention as helping the young person resolve the nature of their sexuality (although progress in this area may occur); rather, it is to help them internalise what represents acceptable forms of sexual behaviour and provide them with strategies that they can use to manage sexual arousal. Such arousal is not always the primary drive for harmful sexual behaviour. But for those children who have established a pattern of abusing, the reinforcing qualities of sex mean that sexual gratification can begin to act as a primary drive.

One particular challenge for the clinician is if the young person becomes sexually aroused during sessions where sexual material is discussed in a relatively direct way. Clinicians should be prepared for this eventuality and have ways of dealing with it. Young adolescent males may experience erections in inappropriate contexts as a matter of course. If this occurs during discussion of sexual material then the clinician may judge that the matter should be acknowledged. It can be helpful to do this in a straightforward manner and acknowledge that it might be difficult or embarrassing to talk about these things with an adult. If appropriate, the clinician may wish to 'normalise' this response and comment that it is not unusual for adolescents to become aroused in this manner. In addition, some young people may expect the clinician to be aroused in a similar way, or to respond in an abusive manner given their prior experiences. It can be helpful for the clinician to state that they are aware of how the young person might be thinking and that this is a safe context in which adults do not behave in that way. In other words, the therapeutic context provides (perhaps for the first time) a setting in which boundaries are observed, and issues of sexuality are dealt with in a responsible and sensitive manner.

Sexual arousal can also sometimes be accompanied by heightened affect, increased distractibility or inappropriate comments. There may be a need to explore how the young person can manage these responses and explore strategies that can help, for example switching focus onto everyday thoughts or images. In Session 3 the adolescent works with the clinician to explicitly develop a set of these strategies. Issues may also arise if there is a history of sexual abuse and discussion of sexual matters may elicit potentially difficult memories alongside feelings of arousal. Acknowledging (and empathising with) difficulties, normalising and switching the focus of the session to different material as a break can help such arousal subside. Finally, the clinician should be aware of how arousal may be linked to risk for the young person. In view of their previous behaviour and current presentation the clinician should on the basis of their clinical formulation make an informed judgement as to the level of risk posed by the heightened arousal prompted by material covered in session. This risk should be addressed by helping the young person identify ways they can manage that arousal safely, ending the session on a neutral topic and if necessary making carers and relevant professionals aware that a heightened level of risk may need to be managed.

Acknowledging early adversity: Helping the young person take responsibility

Session 4 focuses on adverse experiences that the young person has had in their own life. This is not a treatment for trauma, but a space to acknowledge that there may have been times when they have not been cared for or looked after in ways that were acceptable. Prior to exploring the young person's own sense of responsibility for their actions this work is helpful in that it helps to validate their own feelings which, if not acknowledged, can serve to block progress. By helping the young person create a positive narrative about how they coped with adversity in the past places them in a better position to take a constructive stance in relation to their own actions. In other words, they can recognise prior strengths to build on and resolve to act in a way that sets them apart from others who treated them unfairly. It is important to be aware of the level of victimisation that the young person may have experienced and include this in the clinical formulation; the clinician must decide whether this needs additional therapeutic intervention. Such work is beyond the scope of the current manual.

The theme of responsibility first introduced in the Relationships module is revisited from a different angle. As noted in the introduction there are reasons why individuals avoid taking responsibility, and until these are tackled it can be a fruitless endeavour to try to make someone take this step. Avoiding responsibility can be linked to the young person's beliefs about what taking responsibility actually means. Inviting them to explore the pros and cons can shed some light on the beliefs that they hold and the role any denial may be playing in protecting them either in the external world (e.g. avoiding rejection from caregivers) or in their internal world (e.g. avoiding the implication that they are inherently bad). Narcissism is one defence that some adolescents employ. Such defences are not easily shifted – the goal here is to help the young person see themselves as a valuable person despite the unacceptability of their behaviour. Given the often serious consequences of harmful sexual behaviour (for example, removal from home), it is not unlikely that an adolescent has begun to fear that their sense of personal identity (which is highly sensitive at this stage in development) will become dominated by the role of 'abuser'. Such identification arguably is associated with an increased risk of future abusive behaviour. This is a powerful fear that can also be worked with by helping to boost the positive elements of the young person's identity and their achievements. These strategies have the goal of the young person taking a more mature approach to responsibility for their actions.

Putting the young person 'in the driving seat': Making different choices

The final section of the module explores the behavioural choices the young person is likely to have had in the events leading up to their HSB. Again, the goal here is to improve recognition, the time of choice points, as well as to develop their behavioural repertoire by encouraging them to generate alternative responses that will avoid placing themselves in a risk situation. It is useful to link this work with the sexual arousal discussions held earlier in the module by helping the adolescent see that seemingly insignificant choices early on are the best points to make balanced decisions. As they increasingly place themselves in a position of risk, heightened emotional and sexual responses can make balanced decisions more challenging.

Overview of sessions

Session 1: My Feelings

This session represents a shift from exploring the young person's interaction with others to focusing on their own internal world. The goal in this session is to widen their emotional vocabulary as well as their understanding of emotions. Feelings are considered in terms of associated bodily sensations and emotional expressions and the role of thoughts is introduced. Rating scales are used to help the young person begin to calibrate emotions – first in relation to fictional characters and then later in relation to their own feelings.

Session 2: Getting a Handle on My Feelings

This session extends the young person's understanding of feelings. Initially the focus is on the function served by feelings. This is to emphasise the important signalling role that emotions play. Even feelings of anger are important – the challenge is to understand what they are telling us about our situation and how we can best act on them. Fictional vignettes are used to help the young person consider how thoughts can influence how strongly we respond emotionally to situations and how they can help to regulate emotions. Particularly negative thoughts about a situation or attributions to another person can serve to heighten feelings of depression or anger whereas more balanced thoughts can moderate the intensity of negative feelings. Thoughts are considered as 'changing the volume' of our feelings. These ideas are then explored in the context of one of the young person's own experiences.

Session 3: Strategies to Deal with Harmful Sexual Thoughts

This session focuses directly on the issue of abusive sexual thoughts. The young person is first helped to define what constitute abusive sexual thoughts and fantasies – essentially any sexual thoughts about children or which involve force. A clear link is made between these mental experiences and the risk of actual harm behaviour that is further increased by masturbating to such fantasies. Five strategies to deal with such worrying thoughts are presented:

1. escape: avoiding or removing oneself from risk situations
2. saying 'NO!' – mentally rejecting these thoughts
3. taking control: thinking about the bigger picture and the consequences of sexually harming again

4. seeking support: talking to a trusted adult
5. time out: engaging in distracting or alternative safe behaviours that are incompatible with abuse.

The session also includes a discussion helping the young person reflect on why they may be having such thoughts and fantasies, and whether certain behaviours or experiences may have increased their arousal or negative feelings.

Session 4: Dealing with the Past and Facing the Future

This session accommodates the need to think about the young person as a victim – and not just a perpetrator. This balance is one of the main therapeutic challenges in working with these young people who are often cast in one role or the other by the different professionals working around them. The challenge is to engage the adolescent in thinking about their past but avoid dwelling on material that has not been processed and which remains traumatic. It is common that these young people will have had experiences of abuse, domestic violence and chaotic living environments – each of these may provide material for this session. Clinical judgement should be employed to ensure that all material is dealt with in a boundaried and safe manner. The primary aim here is to validate the young person's feelings about their past rather than determine the facts which may or may not have occurred. An additional goal is for the young person to think about how they wish to distinguish themselves from those who behaved in a harmful or unjust way towards them – and, for example, take responsibility for their actions.

Session 5: Taking Responsibility

It is very common for adolescents who have displayed HSB to deny responsibility or partly attribute responsibility for their actions to others. Helping them to adopt a more mature and accurate view of responsibility succeeds best by revisiting the question from time to time over an extended period; this provides space for the young person to reflect and make incremental shifts rather than demonstrating a volte-face which is for many reasons extremely unlikely. The use of the responsibility pie-chart is very useful in this respect to chart progress (and prevent slippage). In this session the question of taking responsibility is introduced in an exploratory context, with the young person encouraged to consider the pros and cons in order to reflect the likely ambivalence that they may feel. A pair of fictional vignettes take the spotlight off the adolescent for part of the session as they consider how other people can make it easier or harder for someone to take responsibility for their actions. Finally, a strength-based approach is used whereby the young person is invited to recall times in the past that they have taken responsibility for their actions. The session ends with the clinician asking the young person to reflect on whether their attitude towards taking responsibility for their HSB has changed.

Session 6: Detective Work – Clues to My HSB

At this point the focus of the work reverts to the external world and the behavioural choices made by the young person in the period leading up to their abusive behaviour. Given that this work can elicit defensiveness it can be helpful to frame it in a neutral way whereby the adolescent themselves takes an objective view of what happened. The nature of the clues are described as 'warning signals' that can help them in the future to spot risk situations and avoid them at an early stage. These signals or clues are categorised as features of the situation and in terms of the thoughts and feelings that they may have had. An important message is that identifying potentially risky situations and choices early on is most likely to keep the young person safe. How this session is focused with regards to time scale will vary depending on the nature of the young person's abusive behaviour. For those with a longer period of grooming and planning, an extended window within which clues are identified would be more appropriate.

There is potentially a great deal of material to cover in this session and it may in fact require two sessions to complete adequately.

A full version of this session as it appears on the CD-ROM is included in the samples section, at the back of this book.

Session 7: Making Better Choices

This session explicitly builds on the last by demonstrating to the young person the opportunity they have – once warning signals have been detected – to make different choices. A fictional vignette is first used to allow them to have an opportunity to identify choices and generate alternative behaviours before progressing to reflect on their own HSB. Across both tasks it is helpful for them to rate how difficult a 'better choice' is at each stage. For most young people it is evident that as their actions increasingly create a context where abuse is possible, and as they become more sexually aroused, it becomes more difficult to make good choices that will keep them safe. The home project provides a further opportunity to develop these skills.

Session 8: Anger Strategies

The work then moves on to consider aggression as one response to anger. The young person will have already begun a consideration of the pros and cons of being aggressive as part of their home project for session 2. The aim here is to foster motivation for change and introduce again the young person's timeline and broader goals. Thinking about how aggression fits into their long term goals can act as a powerful motivator for change. A variety of anger strategies are then introduced (assertiveness, time out, relaxation, a visualisation strategy and perspective taking). There is a great deal of material to be covered here and in fact any one of these strategies could fill a single session. It is therefore important to strike a balance between introducing the range of options available to the young person and spending time on one or two in particular so that they are meaningfully elaborated.

Which strategies are likely to be most effective for each young person is a matter of clinical judgement. For those young people with marked anger control problems additional work here may be required.

MODULE 4: ROAD MAP FOR THE FUTURE – ENDING AND RELAPSE PREVENTION

The work now moves on to the final five sessions. Depending on how many previous sessions have been delivered the clinician may consider that this is the time to consolidate much of the previous work by including the four 'additional' sessions to make up the 30-week programme. A number of suggested sessions are provided here in order to bring the therapy to a close and consolidate and extend previous work. The focus of these sessions, however, will vary a great deal for each young person and the clinician should exercise clinical judgement on a case-by-case basis. This will involve thinking about future relationships and reviewing those aspects of the work that have been most salient for each adolescent in treatment and individualising these ending sessions accordingly. For example, there may be a focus on specific skills (e.g. anger management) alongside a core focus on the concerns for a given adolescent (e.g. sexual attraction to younger children or their feelings of rejection that are associated with HSB). This 'road map' should bring together:

- the new skills that the young person has learnt
- ways in which risk situations can be identified
- key strategies to stay safe
- a list of key social supports.

It is not uncommon for the clinician to feel overwhelmed at the sheer volume of material that could potentially be reviewed and also anxious at the prospect of the young person no longer having the supportive framework provided by the experience of therapy. This is quite natural, and is often accentuated by the prospect of the young person 'going it alone' when there may well still be areas of ongoing concern and vulnerability. There is a need to accept that some level of ongoing risk is inevitable. The task of the clinician is to manage this risk as effectively as possible. This may include use of the following strategies:

- working with the young person's carers and/or social worker to ensure that child protection concerns are adequately addressed at home and at school
- ensuring that the young person has access to support and is provided with real opportunities to develop and grow
- firmly handing over to the young person responsibility for their own behaviour, acknowledging and praising the progress they have achieved

- helping the young person develop a clear road map for the future which highlights both the positive direction they wish to pursue, but also summarises a core 'tool kit' to help them get there
- organising, if appropriate, a limited set of follow-up sessions (typically around four) with the young person over the year following the end of treatment.

There is a need from the outset of this module (if not before) to prepare the young person for the end of therapy. As with termination in any therapeutic relationship, ending will elicit feelings and reactions in the adolescent that will need to be acknowledged and thought about within the clinical session. With adolescents in particular these feelings may not be explicitly articulated but expressed in their behaviour. For example, they may begin to start missing appointments as a way to take control of a situation where they feel they are going to be 'rejected' in any case. It can be helpful to flag up well in advance the number of sessions that are remaining and be clear about any follow-up sessions that are planned. At least one follow-up session is recommended as good practice.

The clinician can acknowledge explicitly that the young person may have ambivalent feelings about ending:

'We now have three sessions left, so it won't be long before we will be at the end of the programme. How do you think you will feel about that? Tell me one thing you will miss about therapy. And tell me one thing you won't miss about coming here every week.'

'You may have some good feelings about not having to come here any more. Some young people can also sometimes feel sad or anxious about stopping therapy. Having mixed feelings is very common. Let's keep an eye on the fact that we are ending soon, and we can continue to think about how to manage it over the next few weeks. How does that sound?'

'We will soon be coming to the end of our work together. How do you think you will feel about that? One way for us to deal with this is if we spend some time thinking about a time when you had to end something before or say goodbye to someone. It may be someone you got to know well, or even leaving your old school. What was that like?'

Taking the young person's own prior experience of endings is a good way to develop a more concrete framework to explore the ambivalent feelings they may be currently having about ending therapy. The young person can feel angry and rejected at the sessions finishing; uncertain, fearful and anxious at the prospect of facing the future on their own; and, at the same time, hugely relieved and joyful at not having to come every week to think about their thoughts and behaviour. Therapists too are likely to have a range of feelings about the therapy coming to an end.

Overview of sessions

Session 1: Healthy Sexual Relationships

The first part of this session covers some basic facts relating to male and female sexual development. In parallel the young person's attitudes to sex and relationships are elicited. Many young people with HSB present with distorted beliefs and attitudes about sex and gender. For example, some adolescents can have extreme views as to how men 'should' behave, the role of women, how a man should deal with his sex drive and so forth. The second half of the session therefore brings the topic firmly into the domain of relationships – the young person reflects on their own experience in order to develop their definition of a 'healthy sexual relationship'.

Session 2: Sexuality and Dating

In this session the focus moves on to issues around sexual attraction, dealing with homosexuality (non-problematic) and sexual attraction to children (problematic). Homosexual feelings can be a delicate issue for some young people unsure of their own identity or struggling to come to terms with sexual abuse from a same sex older young person or adult. These issues need to be handled sensitively. By contrast, clear boundaries should be drawn in relation to sexual attraction towards children. The module ends by building on the practical relationship skills using a role-play task to help develop assertiveness skills.

Session 3: Better Relationships

This session reviews those aspects relevant for helping the young person in initiating and building stable relationships with others. There is a particular focus on situations and relationships that may increase the risk of HSB and a review of strategies that they can adopt to reduce this risk and keep safe.

Session 4: Staying in the Driving Seat

This session focuses on aspects relevant to self-regulation ('staying in the driving seat') beginning with renewing the young person's motivation for change and highlighting their positive future goals. Key 'tools' covered in the Self-Regulation module are reviewed including: managing feelings; anger strategies; sexual arousal strategies; and making better choices. A full version of this session as it appears on the CD-ROM is included in the samples section at the back of the book.

Session 5: Ending Therapy – Looking towards the Future

The final session is to draw the therapy to a close and help the young person identify the ways in which they are able to better meet their aspirations and goals across different domains and avoid the risk of harming others sexually in the future. The (often ambivalent) feelings they may have about ending are also explored. It can be helpful in some cases to provide the young person with a certificate to acknowledge the work they have completed.

Appendix I:
Sample Session Plans and Home Projects

Engagement Module

Session 1: Making an Authentic Connection

> **CORE AIMS**
>
> - To begin to establish a collaborative therapeutic relationship
> - To explicitly acknowledge and explore why the young person has come for therapy
> - To help the young person articulate how they would like their life to change.

OVERVIEW OF THE SESSION

The session comprises three main tasks:

1. Establish with the young person why they have come for therapy.
2. Introduce the therapy, nature of the sessions and the work.
3. Begin to set positive goals for the future.

This first session may benefit from allocating 1 hour and 15 minutes (rather than the usual hour) to ensure that the key tasks are covered. Remember that by the end of the session you want to have achieved the three core aims. Obviously there are many potential questions you might ask and information about the therapy you can give; these considerations should be balanced against whether or not they assist in meeting the core aims of the session.

1. INTRODUCTION

Setting the scene

It can be helpful if the opening remarks include both a relational or empathic element acknowledging that the YP is meeting you for the first time as well as an expression of warmth – being pleased that the YP has come. For example you might say:

'This first session is a chance for me to tell you a bit about our work together and understand how you see things. I guess it can often be difficult meeting with someone you don't know for the first time. But I am really pleased that you have come along today. Does that make sense? Can I start by asking you first why you are here?'

> ## TIPS ON SCENE SETTING
>
> The first session sets the tone and establishes in the mind of the YP a powerful set of expectations as to the nature of the intervention. There is considerable individual variability in how young people present in their first session. While many are anxious and uncertain, these feelings can be presented in very different ways ranging from being withdrawn to aggressive. The challenge is to establish rapport and at the same time convey a sense of confidence and credibility. Be prepared for dealing with non-compliance and oppositional behaviour.
>
> Remember that establishing rapport and trust takes time and is a cumulative task to be achieved over the course of the intervention. Initially the YP is likely to be mistrustful and reserved. At this stage you should endeavour to model a collaborative interaction by:
>
> - seeking the young person's views
> - providing opportunities for their input to shape the session
> - demonstrating a straightforward and honest approach
> - reflecting back concerns and ambivalence as appropriate
> - having a non-judgemental and transparent approach to non-communication by the YP.

Why is the young person here?: Eliciting their view

Exploring with the YP why they think they are here is a central task in this first session. It is important to address this issue at the beginning for a number of reasons. It demonstrates that you are able to acknowledge and articulate the issue of their HSB in a matter of fact and straightforward way; many young people will have experienced professionals who have avoided addressing the issue head on. Second, naming the problem behaviour can actually serve to reduce anxiety (for you and the YP). Third, a clear message is conveyed as to a core purpose of the intervention.

> *'It would be helpful for me to have an idea what you think – why do you think we are here today?'*

Typically the YP will not be very forthcoming. One example exchange might go like this:

> *T: It would be helpful for me to have an idea what you think – why do you think we are here today?*
>
> *YP: I am here to get help because of the problems I had.*
>
> *T: What kind of problems?*
>
> *YP: Hmm… problems with my behaviour.*
>
> *T: Okay, so you are here to get help with your behaviour problems. What specific behaviour problems have you had?*
>
> *YP: Do you mean what kinds of behaviour? … Sexual behaviour I suppose.*
>
> *T: And what problems have you had with your sexual behaviour?*
>
> *YP: Hmm… I dunno.*
>
> *T: Can you tell me what you did that people are worried about?*
>
> *YP: I suppose I accidentally touched someone.*
>
> *T: Okay, just so I get this right – you are here to get help with your sexual behaviour because you touched someone. Is that right? What do people call that, when someone touches another person sexually when they shouldn't?*
>
> *YP: Abuse maybe, I'm not sure.*
>
> *T: That's right – this kind of behaviour is sexual abuse. Well done for being clear about this – it is important to be able to be honest. If we are not clear what the problems are then it will be much harder to try and solve them. You are the expert on yourself and what is going on in your own head so I need you to tell me what you think. Does that make sense?*

Not all young people will be so articulate as the client in this case example. If a YP is not so forthcoming it can be helpful to reflect back what they have said (e.g. *'It sounds like your foster carer is concerned about some things that have happened'*) and to ask *'I wonder if you can tell me a little bit more about that'*.

- It can also be helpful to explore the YP's perception of the problem by asking them about the view of a significant other: *'If your mum/social worker/foster carer/teacher/a judge was here, what do you think they would say their concerns were?'*

- The YP may disagree or be dismissive of the views of others. You may wish to say: '*It sounds like you have some concerns about what your social worker thinks. Tell me about that.*'
- You may wish to explore the YP's perception of how therapy might work: '*So how do you see therapy being able to help you? Do you think it might?*'

The important thing at this stage is to take an active listening stance. At this stage the need to name the core issue as to why the YP is in therapy needs to be balanced with the risk of evoking powerful feelings of shame which have the potential to close down communication altogether. While you can reflect back what the YP says and ask open questions to elicit more information it is good to proceed quite briskly through this section. If the YP is able to state some (correct) reasons for why they are here, reinforce that ('*It is very good that you are able to be honest about that; talking about these things can sometimes be difficult*'). Some level of denial, avoidance and minimisation is extremely common – be reassured that this is a key issue that will be addressed subsequently during the intervention.

Why is the young person here?: Stating your view

After this stage clearly state *your* understanding of why the YP is there (this is not a question). For example:

> '*My understanding is that there are concerns about your sexually harmful behaviour – and that in the past you sexually abused X. We won't be focusing on that today but it helps us understand why we are here.*'

> '*The aim of our work is for you to show only positive sexual behaviours in the future and generally feel good about yourself.*'

> '*I have worked with a lot of young people in your situation, and there are plenty of things we can work on together to make that happen.*'

> '*How does that sound?*'

The young person will almost certainly have some feelings about speaking about their HSB and this is an opportune moment to engage in some mentalising work. For example, it can be helpful to pause at this point and acknowledge or check out what the YP might be feeling:

> '*My guess is that you probably didn't like my mentioning the sexual abuse. If that's the case, it would be useful if you could tell me when I say things that you don't like…*'

> '*It's not always possible to avoid talking about things that are uncomfortable or worrying. I can't promise that but I want to go at your pace and to learn to see things from your point of view as much as I can.*'

> '*So one of the rules of coming to see me is that you can always tell me if we are going too fast. How are we doing now? Does this seem okay?*'

2. INTRODUCING THE THERAPY

How the sessions work

Here briefly provide an overview of what therapy is likely to entail ('*Okay, let me start by giving you a bit of information about what we do here*'). At this point in the session you might want to cover some general issues about the therapy, including:

- describing who you are
- explaining that there will be X [number of] sessions, lasting for 60 minutes each
- saying where the sessions will take place
- commenting on privacy and confidentiality
- describing whether there will be changes in therapist (which can arise if two therapists are working jointly to deliver the treatment)
- introducing the idea of project work that the YP completes outside the sessions
- highlighting the importance of attendance and what the YP should do if they cannot come.

Ground rules

When introducing the discussion of ground rules there is a risk of losing a collaborative rapport and overloading the YP with information. To reduce the likelihood of this it can be useful to ask the YP what they think the ground rules should be. What rules do they follow with their social worker? What rules will help the therapy go well? It can be useful to identify *respect* as a core rule – the need to respect one another as a person. Other rules may relate to what the YP can bring into the room, taking drinks/eating, being honest and so forth. You may wish to write up a list of ground rules on the flip-chart.

'Do you have any questions for me?'

It can be helpful to acknowledge that in this session, because you are explaining about the treatment programme, you have to do more talking than usual. The typical structure of the therapy session is covered in the next session to reduce the amount of information being conveyed at this stage.

3. GOALS FOR THE FUTURE

This final task can be covered briskly and is a positive way to end the session. The task is continued in the home project, so there is no need to ensure that it is completed in the session itself, but it works well to end the session on this positive note.

'Today we are going to finish off by thinking about the future.'

[Go up to the wall where you have your blank timeline pages already prepared.]

'Let's imagine this is your life [begin drawing a horizontal line]. *Let's mark here when you were born...* [add in date of birth; then two thirds of the way across, draw one line going upwards at 45° – where the line changes direction draw a circle] *...and this is now.'* Invite the YP up to the timeline and hand them the marker; having them actively mark the timeline themselves is a powerful way to promote an active engagement in the session.

'So this chart is called a timeline. Later we will be thinking more about the past, but for now I want you to think about your future. We could look, say, at your future in one year [mark this age on the line] *and even five years* [mark age].*'*

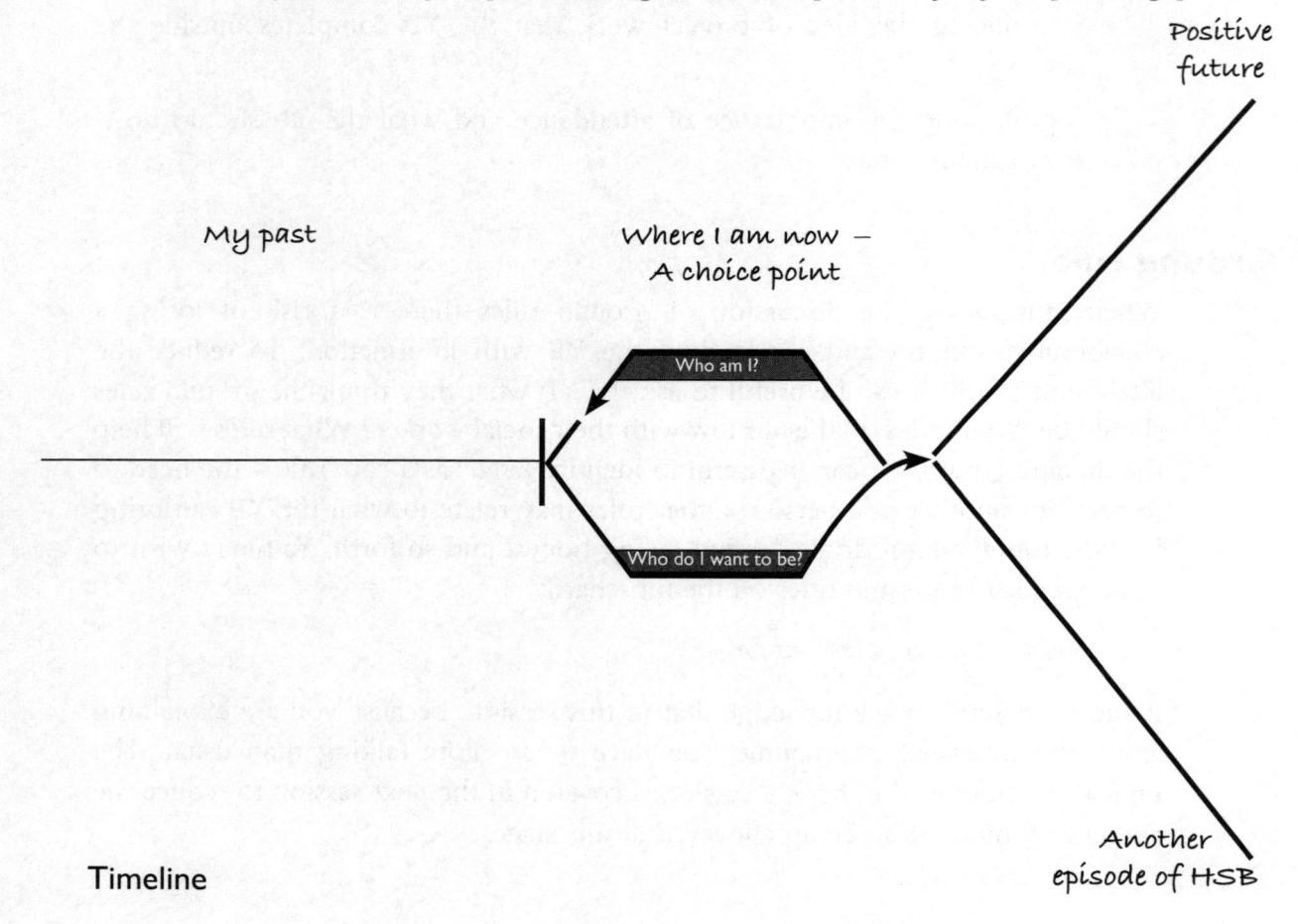

My past | Where I am now – A choice point | Positive future

Who am I?

Who do I want to be?

Another episode of HSB

Timeline

Explain to the young person that you would like them to think about how they would like things to be different in the future. Begin by looking to one year from now:

> *'Looking forward one year from now, how would you like your life to be different at the end of this programme?'*

> *'If things could be different, what would they be like?'*

> *'What changes do you want to see in yourself, as a person?'*

Help them to consider different aspects of their lives including:

- new skills or attitudes
- what they will be doing (school/college/job)
- their social context (friends)
- where they might be living (home life)
- what their interests might be (activities or hobbies – usually things they are too young to do now).

If there are concrete examples, invite the YP to go up and write these on the positive arm of the timeline. These can be elaborated in future weeks; however, be mindful of those young people who may not feel very confident or indeed may be anxious about their level of literacy, and who may be unsure of how to spell the words they wish to write. Young people often need help to explore and expand their expectations for the future. They might say for example they want to go to university: *What will they study? What will a typical day be like for them? What kind of things might they do at the weekend?*

Having the YP working at the flip-chart or on the timeline also shifts the direct focus away from the adolescent; instead a joint and more collaborative interaction is created by the therapist and the YP having a neutral focus for their attention. Give positive feedback – but be careful to praise in a low key (even humorous) way as adolescents can be sensitive to overt adult praise.

4. HOME PROJECT

> *'For the home project this week I want you to do some more thinking about how you would like things to be different in the future. Here is a profile – like one you would have online. Imagine that you are writing it five years from now. I want you to think about each of the four sections we have talked about today and write a short description in each…and we can talk about them next week. How does that sound? Do you have any questions?'*

5. FEEDBACK

'Okay – so we are nearly finished for today. At the end of each session I will ask you how you think it went. So for today's session tell me something that you think went well. Or something that you enjoyed.'

'...And what about something that wasn't so useful or that you found a bit harder?'

It is important to help facilitate honest feedback, which can include negative comments. These few moments at the end of the session are a chance for the young person to express their views and feelings. These should be acknowledged by the therapist and ideally used to inform how future sessions are delivered. For example: *'It sounds as though you enjoyed working on the board. Let's think in the later sessions how we can do more of that'*; *'It sounds like it was difficult to talk about abusing Jack; you did very well today to acknowledge that'*. You may wish to introduce the idea of 'guessing' how the young person might have experienced the session. For example: *'I guess you might have found it difficult meeting a new person today and talking about some pretty tricky things. Would that be right?'* This demonstrates mentalisation on behalf of the clinician and shows you have a curiosity and interest in their experience.

HOME PROJECT 1: MAPPING MY FUTURE

In this week's home project you need to do some more thinking about how you would like things to be different in the future. Here is a profile – like one you would have online. Imagine that you are writing it five years from now.

Write your name in the box in the centre. Then think about each of the four sections and write a short description in each. You can then discuss your 'future profile' in session next week.

Job/college: In this section describe what you would like to be doing. This might be a job or studying at college. Try to give as much detail as possible and say why you enjoy it.

Friends: What kind of friends would you like in five years' time? You might have some old friends and new friends. Describe them.

Free time: What are your hobbies? What do you like to do in your spare time? These might be things you are not able or allowed to do at the moment or need to be older to do.

Travel: Where would you like to travel to in the future? What kinds of places appeal to you? Imagine where you would like to go and describe your travels here.

| My job/ College | My friends |

| My free time | My travel |

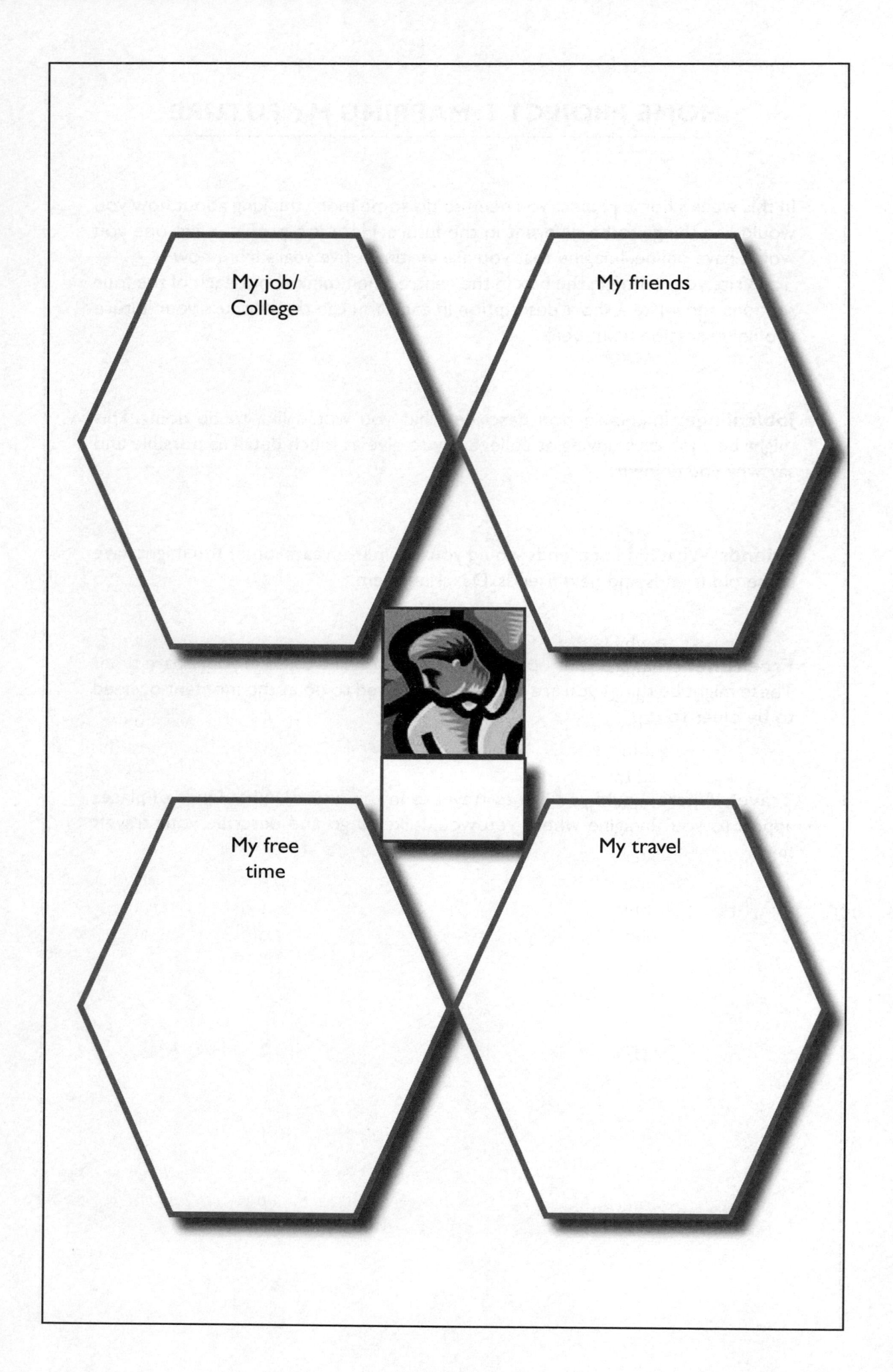

110

Relationships Module

Session 2: Taking Responsibility

CORE AIMS

- To explicitly explore the young person's harmful sexual behaviour
- To map out the young person's harmful sexual behaviour timeline
- To engage the young person in thinking about responsibility.

OVERVIEW OF THE SESSION

The first part of this session focuses on creating a mini-timeline which provides the basis to explore the YP's HSB and their (often distorted) understanding of what happened and why. At this stage of the intervention a more stable alliance with the YP should allow some direct questions to be asked. The task in this session is not to help the YP re-evaluate what happened but first to elicit as clear a picture as possible of the events associated with their HSB. In the second part of the session you should engage the YP in thinking about who was responsible for what happened. A responsibility pie-chart is used to capture the YP's perspective in visual form. A number of strategies can then be adopted to help the YP re-evaluate their position, with the intention that they will be better able to take responsibility themselves. Work on responsibility is continued in later sessions.

Note that you may wish to consider allocating two sessions to cover adequately the tasks presented here. The mini-timeline is a key element and so too is the work in relation to responsibility. Depending on the YP either one of these may take a session in itself.

1. WEEKLY REVIEW – SETTING THE AGENDA – HOME PROJECT

Check on the YP's week and then introduce the theme of the session.

'Today we are going to move on and start thinking about what happened when you sexually harmed X. We will create a mini-timeline and talk about who you think was responsible for what happened. So, for this week the agenda will look like this:'

> **Beginning**
>
> Review of the week – Home project
>
> **Main tasks**
>
> What happened
>
> Taking responsibility
>
> **Ending**
>
> New home project – Issues to discuss – Feedback

'Is there anything you would like to discuss or add to the agenda this week?'

Look over the YP's home project work. Explore with them how they found the task. As usual, praise effort made and explore their responses. Try to elicit from the YP what they have learnt from doing the task. Their responses to this task can be important when thinking about risk and relapse prevention – is the YP staying over with friends who have younger children? Are they in contact with other young people who they have targeted in the past? Are they being bullied, and do they feel socially isolated? Do they find it easy to make friends with peers? This important information can help you best focus the content of subsequent sessions.

2. MY RELATIONSHIP WITH MY VICTIM: WHAT HAPPENED

> *'So far we have been thinking about relationships and how we can handle them better. The main reason why you are here is because of your relationship with [the victim] and so it will be important for us also to think about that relationship. I have worked with a lot of young people who have showed the same kind of behaviour, so I hope you can be honest with me. We have started to get to know each other over the last few weeks, I think, and that can help when we talk about difficult things. I won't be shocked or annoyed with you. Does that sound okay? Do you have any questions?'*

> '*Maybe a good place to start might be for you to tell me a little more about what happened. I know this is something that you might have some worries about: that is pretty normal. But a simple way of doing things is for us to create a mini-timeline. This is something we can add to as you remember new things. I have put on the wall a blank timeline for you to fill in. As you can see it focuses on the time when you sexually abused* [insert name of victim].'

> '*I want you to think back to that day…and tell me about what was happening.*'

It may not be helpful to focus on exploring the YP's feelings about talking through their HSB as this may simply increase arousal and the risk of dysregulation. Rather, you should try to proceed in a contained and matter-of-fact way to obtain the details of what happened. First elicit details from the YP about what they were doing that day. Where were they? Who was around? What happened? In addition, you can elicit how the YP was feeling and if possible what they were thinking. Events can go below the line and thoughts and feelings can be placed above the line (see the case example below).

> '*Okay, I want you to tell me what was happening the hour* (week/day/morning) *before the incident.*' Again, add these details to the timeline in note form.

> '*So now I want you to tell me about how you abused* [name of victim].' Consider including questions such as these here:

- Where were you?
- Who were you with?
- What were you doing?
- What were you thinking?
- What was happening to your body?
- What were you feeling?
- What did [*name of victim*] do or say?
- What did you do next?

The YP, especially if this is the first time that the HSB incident is explored in session, is likely to be reticent and unwilling to give details, and may minimise, distort and indeed deny what occurred. It is important for you to realise that this is only the start of a process that should continue over the course of therapy; in other words, the mini-timeline can be elaborated in future sessions as new information emerges. By asking relevant questions, eliciting and recording necessary material and challenging any distorted thinking in a balanced but clear way, a cumulative narrative of the incident can be created and recorded visually. Lines of questioning might include:

- How old was the victim? How old were you? How tall was he or she? How tall were you? What did you do so that [*name of victim*] did what you wanted?

    Here it can be helpful to establish with the YP if there was a power imbalance and what the YP did to ensure compliance. You might state: '*So it sounds like you were much older than* [victim] *and also much taller than them. Is that right?*'

- What did you do? What happened as a result? How did they react? What were you thinking and why?

    Here it is important to elicit the actual actions of the YP. These are likely to be described in euphemistic terms. It is important to challenge distorted or vague descriptions. For example: '*So, what you are saying is that you put your penis into* [victim's] *bottom? Is that right? Was your penis hard or soft? … Okay, that's a new piece of information, let's put it on the timeline. When did your penis first get hard? What thoughts were in your mind at that time? What were you feeling at that time?*' In other words, do not collude with the YP's minimisation but feed back what occurred in clear terms, and check the accuracy with the YP.

    The case example contains a number of examples of distorted thinking to be taken up later (e.g. '*I asked him and he said it was okay*'; '*It only happened once*').

- What did you do next?

    Did the YP threaten or bribe the victim? How did he behave after the abuse? How, eventually, was the abuse discovered?

End the task by expressing approval to the YP for working hard on this issue and praising the details that they have managed to put on the timeline. You might want to use an emotional metaphor that it can be 'a bit like having a difficult emotional workout'. A careful judgement needs to be made about how much you acknowledge the YP's feelings at this point. As noted earlier, such prompting can simply serve to heighten the level of emotional responses from the YP and impair their ability to think about responsibility (a more cognitive task) in the next section. Usually, it is best to wait until the end of the session before reflecting with the YP on how they have found doing the tasks.

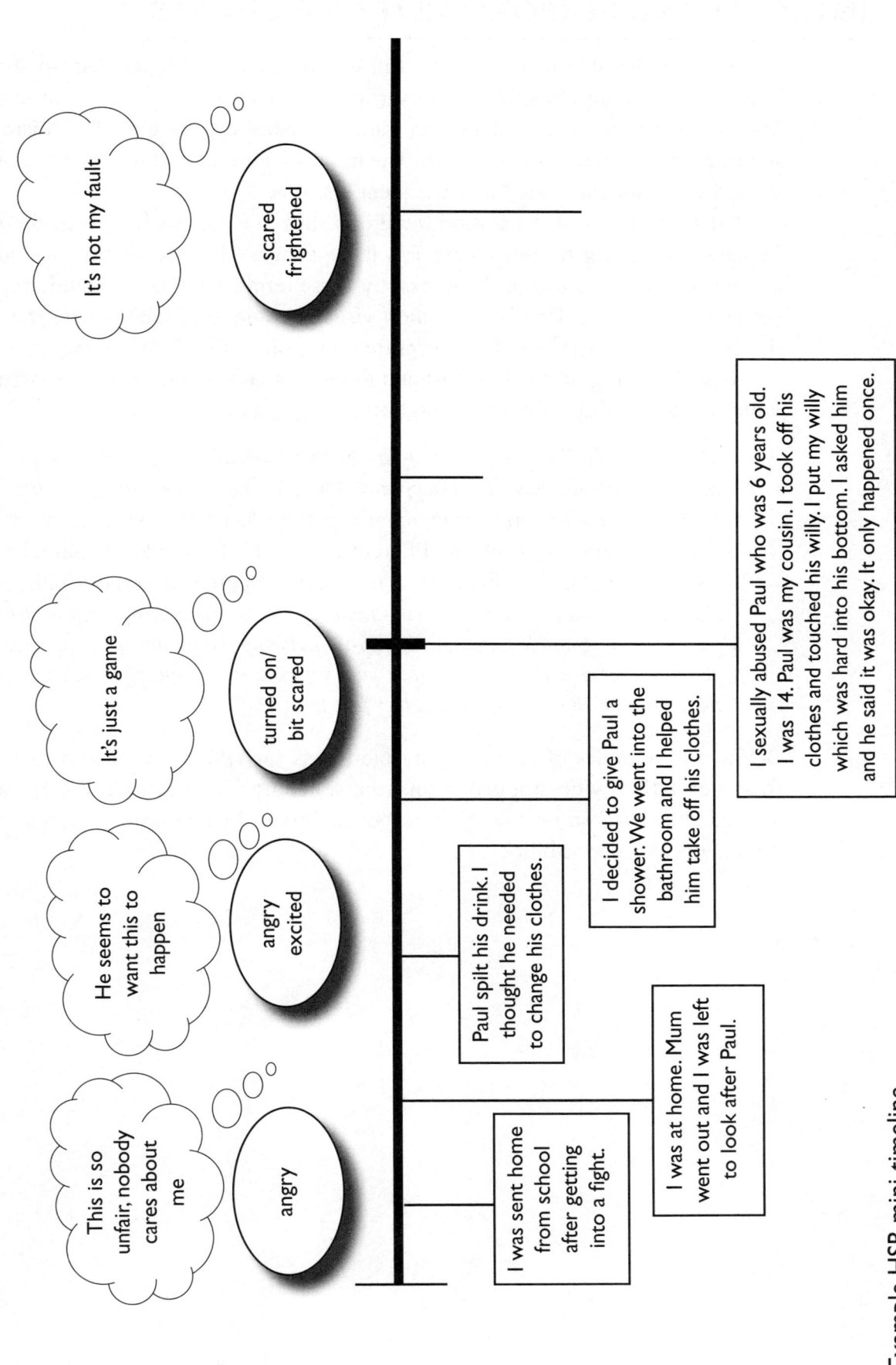

Thoughts (clouds): This is so unfair, nobody cares about me — He seems to want this to happen — It's just a game — It's not my fault

Feelings (ovals): angry — angry / excited — turned on / bit scared — scared / frightened

Events (timeline boxes):
- I was sent home from school after getting into a fight.
- I was at home. Mum went out and I was left to look after Paul.
- Paul spilt his drink. I thought he needed to change his clothes.
- I decided to give Paul a shower. We went into the bathroom and I helped him take off his clothes.
- I sexually abused Paul who was 6 years old. I was 14. Paul was my cousin. I took off his clothes and touched his willy. I put my willy which was hard into his bottom. I asked him and he said it was okay. It only happened once.

Example HSB mini-timeline

3. UNDERSTANDING WHAT HAPPENED: INTRODUCING RESPONSIBILITY PIE-CHARTS

You will not be able to complete a full version of the HSB incident in the first half of the session. Hopefully, however, the core elements can be in put in place. You will have also had a chance to gauge to what degree the YP is distorting, minimising or denying their actions. The mini-timeline should stay on the wall and be added to and elaborated in subsequent sessions.

The second half of the session requires a shift in emphasis from recording *what* happened to trying to understand *why* it happened. The goal of this second task should be presented to the YP in exactly these terms. Here, you should employ a pie-chart technique. This is a common visual technique in CBT where the client divides up a pie-chart in order to capture their point of view on a given question.

Begin by going to the flip-chart and drawing a large circle. At the top write the word 'Responsibility'. You might say something like:

> *'Okay, I would like you to come up to the chart. We are going to go use a pie-chart to help understand what happened. This pie I have called 'Responsibility'. First, can you tell me who are the different people whose fault it was?* [In other words, generate a list of the different people the YP thinks should take responsibility before beginning to allocate degree of responsibility.] *Now, I want you to take the pen and divide up the pie showing how much each person was responsible for what happened. Divide up the pie and write up each person's name in each slice. Let's start with who was most responsible. Who was that? How much of the pie should they take up etc.?'*

Below are examples of responsibility pie-charts for HSB – in relation to the YP, their step-father (who stopped them from watching TV) and Jack, his 4-year-old victim. The charts show change in responsibility at the beginning and end of the discussion on responsibility.

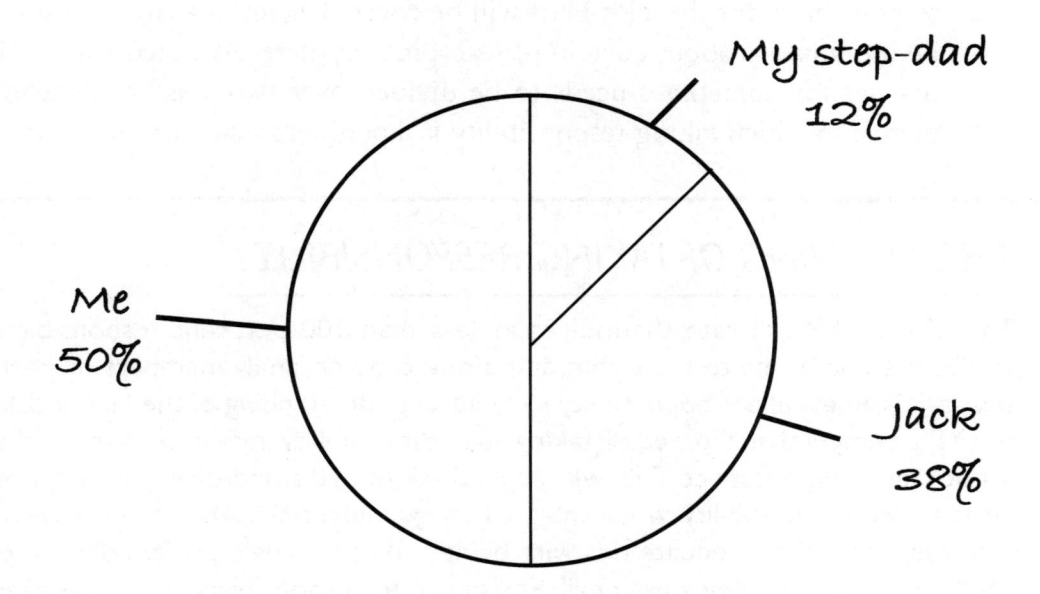

Appendix I: Sample Session Plans and Home Projects 117

My step-dad
12%

Me
50%

Jack
38%

Responsibility Chart: At the start of the discussion on responsibility

My step-dad
3%

Me
65%

Jack
32%

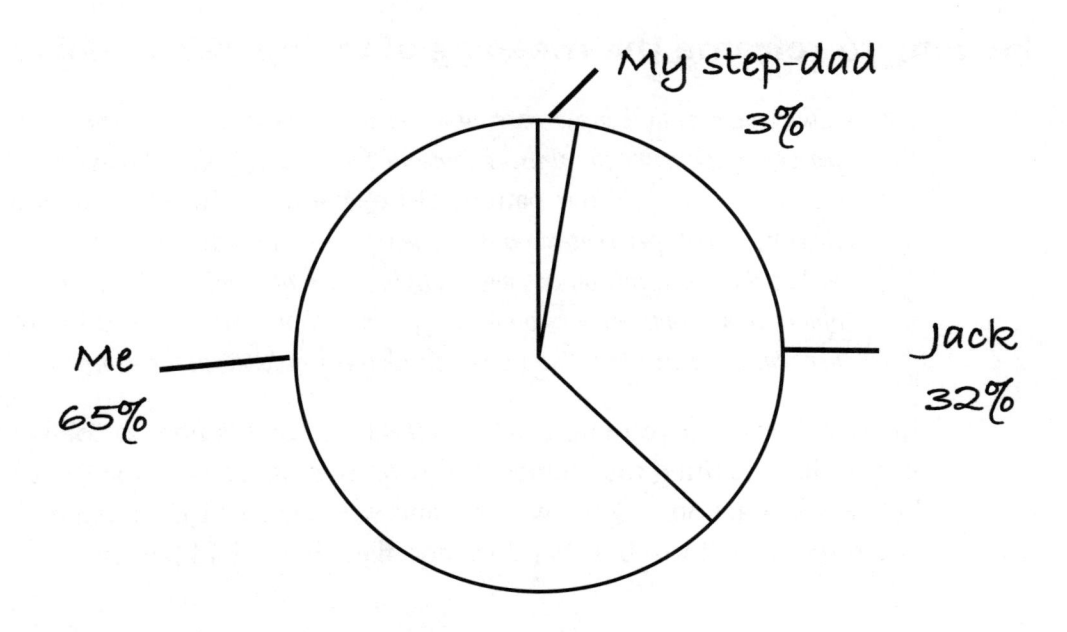

Responsibility Chart 2: At the end of the discussion on responsibility

As time allows, it can be useful to explore these ratings with the YP. The issue of responsibility for the YP's HSB will be covered again in a later session – so do not be too anxious about covering this topic fully here. As noted earlier, the work in this session sometimes needs to be divided over two sessions depending on the degree to which taking responsibility is a pertinent issue for the YP in treatment.

> ### THE MEANING OF TAKING RESPONSIBILITY
>
> Typically the YP will rate themselves as less than 100 per cent responsible and will attribute some blame to the victim, and often to other family members or peers. While this task is an excellent opportunity to build an understanding of the HSB incident from the YP's perspective the act of taking full responsibility may represent a challenging if not traumatic prospect. This will depend on the YP's underlying assumptions as to what taking responsibility would mean. For example, a YP who states 'I was 100 per cent responsible' may equate this with being and remaining a profoundly bad person, a paedophile, or sometimes even evil. Resistance to responsibility therefore needs to be seen in the context of the *function* that it might be playing psychologically – as a defence or coping strategy.

Addressing the issue of responsibility can proceed in the following two ways:

Helping to reframe the meaning of taking responsibility

> *'Okay, here is another pie-chart of a boy named Tony. He has rated himself as 100 per cent responsible for abusing someone the same age as* [insert name of victim and describe a similar pattern of behaviour as the YP in treatment]. *So if Tony is 100 per cent responsible, what does that mean about him as a person? What do you think other people might think of him? What would be so bad about being completely responsible? Do you think this would make Tony a 100 per cent bad person? What do you think this would mean for Tony in the future?'*

In your discussion you might tell the YP that Tony is now at college and is doing very well. One thing that helped Tony was that he realised that there is a difference between our actions – what we do – and who we are. Tony did a bad thing that he was responsible for – but that does not make him a bad person.

Challenging the role of others in the HSB

In relation to the victim, it is important to ask a series of questions that may allow a shift in the level of responsibility accorded to them. After each set of questions revisit the rating the YP has given to the victim and hopefully adjust downwards their attribution of responsibility. For example, you might explore the following:

Disparity in age

You could ask questions such as:

- How old were they?
- Do you think a child at that age is able to decide that they want to have sex?
- What is the legal age at which a person can consent to sex?…So, in the eyes of the law he/she cannot be responsible – is that right?

Disparity in size

Questions might include:

- How tall were they?…How tall were you?
- So it seems like you were a lot taller/bigger. How easy would it have been for them to say no?
- Imagine you were in a room with a much taller and older man who wanted to do something you didn't – how would that make you feel?
- So do you think it is possible that [*victim*] didn't want you to abuse them but they were too scared or frightened to say no?

Misreading cues

Questions could include:

- So, whose idea was it?
- What did [*victim*] say/do that made you think they wanted to have sex with you?
- What else could that have meant?
- So, it sounds like they may not have been wanting to have sex with you at all – is that right?

Conclude this set of questions by asking the YP to look at their ratings again. What do they think now in relation to the victim's level of responsibility? *'Okay – let's look at our ratings again for them. What do you think now – that it would be a little less or the same?'* Write up the new number reflecting the victim's responsibility and add the shift number to the YP's score, giving a new level for their responsibility.

In relation to other people rated as partly responsible it is important to ask a series of questions that can allow the YP to re-evaluate their role. Obviously, the kinds of questions you should ask will depend on their identity and their relationship with the YP. For example, you might ask:

- Were they in the room?
- What did they tell you to do/how did you know they wanted you to do this?
- Is that what they/the police/a judge would say?

- So who was in charge of your body? You put your willy into [*victim*]'s bottom – did you do that or did they do that?

'So, it sounds as if [insert name of person] *didn't actually tell you to abuse* [victim] *and that they weren't even in the room. You've also said that your brain was in charge of your body, not them. I wonder what this means for your rating. Before, you rated them as X per cent responsible. What do you think now?'*

Again, conclude this set of questions by noting by what percentage there has been a shift in responsibility (even 1 per cent is a shift) and write up the new number reflecting the other person's responsibility and add the shift number to the YP's score, giving a new level for their responsibility.

4. ISSUES TO DISCUSS

Issues or incidents raised by the YP.

5. SUMMARY AND HOME PROJECT

Ask the YP how they found the session overall and what they have learnt. Then provide a succinct summary of what has been covered in the session. Introduce the home project 'Taking responsibility for my achievements'. This task is an important reminder for the YP of the things about themselves that they can be proud of and a way for them to think about responsibility in a different context.

6. FEEDBACK

Obtain feedback in the usual way and bring the session to a close.

HOME PROJECT 2:
TAKING RESPONSIBILITY FOR MY ACHIEVEMENTS

In this week's session you thought a lot about taking responsibility in relation to your harmful sexual behaviour. For this home project you need to think of two examples of achievements in your life that you are proud of. These might be all kinds of things; for example:

- winning a football match
- doing a good essay at school
- buying someone a great present
- performing in a band
- going travelling on your own.

For each achievement you need to complete a responsibility pie-chart. Think about who was responsible. Obviously there will be a big part that was your responsibility. But you need to think about who helped you get there. Who brought you to football practice and bought you the kit to help build up your skills?

You might find that you were 85 per cent responsible but two or three other people helped you in all sorts of ways and without them you might not have achieved what you did. Show this on the pie-chart by dividing it up with bigger slices for the people who were more responsible. Give the percentage number for each person and write this in each slice. The example below shows how a finished pie-chart might look.

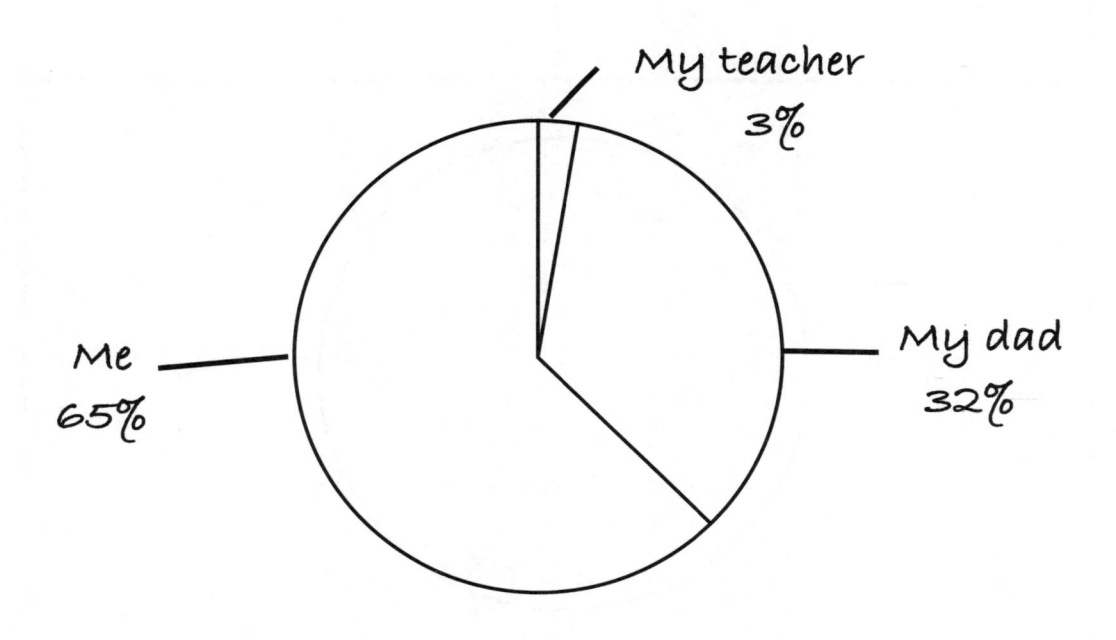

My teacher 3%

Me 65%

My dad 32%

Achievement 1

What you did

Who helped you achieve this?

How did they help you?

Achievement 2

What you did

Who helped you achieve this?

How did they help you?

Self-Regulation Module

Session 6: Detective Work – Clues to My HSB

> **CORE AIMS**
>
> - To help the young person identify risk factors associated with their harmful sexual behaviour
> - To work with the young person to generate strategies to lower risk.

OVERVIEW OF THE SESSION

Note that the material covered in this session is an important part of the therapy programme and can easily fill two sessions. The work opens with an optional task relevant for those YP who may have difficulty taking responsibility for their HSB and who appear to hold negative beliefs about themselves. It essentially aims to help the YP distinguish between their behaviour and their value as a person. The main focus of the session, however, is to identify the set of risk factors preceding the YP's HSB. The material is described as doing detective work to identify 'clues'. These clues are described as warning signals for the YP and can be thoughts, feelings or situations. Each signal is defined as something which made it easier for them to sexually harm. The dual aim is both to identify these warning signals and to generate strategies that the YP could use in the future to respond to those signals.

1. WEEKLY REVIEW – SETTING THE AGENDA – HOME PROJECT

As usual, briefly review how the YP's week has been and go over their home project. Check if there are any issues that need to be brought back for discussion later in the session. Explain that in this session the focus is identifying clues that seem to be linked to their HSB.

> *'Today we are going to do some detective work – and find clues that signal you are at risk of harmful sexual behaviour. This will mean looking at the past and thinking about thoughts, feelings and situations that happened before you sexually harmed and thinking how you can learn from them.'*

> # Beginning
> Review of the week – Home project
>
> # Main tasks
> Optional task: What my HSB means about me
>
> Detective work: Clues about my SHB
>
> # Ending
> New home project – Issues to discuss – Feedback

'Is there anything you would like to discuss or add to the agenda this week?'

2. OPTIONAL TASK: WHAT MY HSB MEANS ABOUT ME

If it emerged in previous sessions that the YP is ambivalent about taking responsibility because of what it will mean about them then this is a short and helpful task to help them re-evaluate that assumption.

'I want to start by spending a few minutes thinking about how you feel about yourself having sexually harmed [victim].'

Draw two rating scales (0–10) up on the flip-chart. Above the first one write 'Action rating' and above the second one write 'Person rating'. First ask the YP to rate how bad they think that their actions were in sexually harming [*insert name of victim*] with 0 being not bad at all and 10 being extremely bad. Then ask the YP to rate how bad they think they are as a person. If the YP rates themselves as 1 or above this should be challenged. As part of this explore the assumptions the YP has about how their behaviour and how they feel about themselves are related. Some possible questions include:

- You have rated your HSB as X – do you think this has affected your rating Y that you are a bad person?

- What about all the positive things you have done in the past, and hope to do in the future? (List some examples if possible.) How do these fit with your rating about yourself as someone who is a bad person?

- What rating would your best friend/close family member (with whom the YP has a positive relationship) give you if we asked them? (Ask them to mark this.) What does that tell you?

- What does this mean? It looks like we can do something bad, but this action doesn't make us a bad person – it doesn't make us who we are. Our actions – and what we take responsibility for – are different from who we are. Does that make sense?

3. DETECTIVE WORK: CLUES ABOUT MY HSB

This task aims to elaborate the timeline of the YP's harmful sexual behaviour that was first sketched out in the Relationships module. The aim is not to repeat the discussion that took place in that module but to:

- add further details to the timeline
- reframe the meaning of each element as a 'warning signal'
- identify strategies to respond to these signals.

The central goal is to help the YP become more aware of the nature and significance of their behaviours and thoughts in order to help them make more informed choices in the future. You might use the following to introduce the rationale:

> '*Okay, now we are going to do a little detective work. You remember we did a mini-timeline before for your HSB? Well, we are going to go back to that now and think a bit more about what happened. We are going to play detectives in a way and look for clues. What you will see is that these clues are actually warning signals that made it easier for you to sexually harm. If you can spot these warning signals in the future, and have ways to respond to them, then you are going to be safer.*'

Work through the following domains using a prepared sheet: situations, thoughts and feelings (see the worked examples below). These at times overlap – that should not be a concern. Simply place each point in the section that seems the most natural fit. It can be helpful to start with some open questions to begin the discussion:

- I want you to think back to the time when you were about to abuse [*insert name of victim*]. Can you think of any warning signs that you noticed?
- Were there any things that helped make it easier to abuse [*insert name of victim*]?
- At what point did you know that you were going to abuse? What were the things that told you that?

.... clues

Signals

1.

2.

3.

4.

Strategies

1.

2.

3.

4.

Easier   Harder

1..2..3..4..5..6..7..8..9..10

Clues template

Situation clues

Characteristics of the context and situation are a good place to start as these can feel less threatening to the YP. The aim is to identify aspects of the situation that facilitated the abuse and at the same time think about how these could inform strategies that would reduce risk of HSB in the future. Situations and environments preceding the HSB often are partly created by the YP – the implication of this is that noticing and anticipating high risk situations should lead to the YP developing not only 'getting out of' but also 'not getting into' strategies; making better choices at earlier stages is the focus of the next session. In the list of situation clues, include not only features of the situation at the time of the HSB but others that you think may be relevant (e.g. looking at pornography, using drugs, being alone with children etc).

> *'Okay, let's start with thinking about the situation and what was happening at the time of your HSB.'*

- You said you were having a bath/at home alone with victim (etc). What was it about that situation that made it easier for [HSB] to occur?
- Was there anything about *where* you were that made it easier/that made it harder to stop yourself doing what you did?
- What if you had been at school/at home with your parents – would it have been more or less likely to happen then? Why?
- What was it about where the abuse happened that made it easier (e.g. isolated, no adults present, private)?
- On a scale of 1–10 with 1 being nearly impossible to abuse [*insert name of victim*] and 10 being very easy, how easy did that situation make it for you?
- If you could change the situation in any way to make it harder for you to have carried out the abuse, what would you change?
- Let's just say that happened – how much more difficult would that have made carrying out the abuse? Which number would you choose now?
- Can you think of any other things you would change about the situation to make it even harder for you/make your rating even lower?
- Thinking back to the day/weeks/months before the abuse, can you think of anything that you did that made it easier for you to abuse?
- More generally – what would be other high risk situations (e.g. looking at pornography on the internet, being alone with young children, being in a job or role where you are responsible for young children)?
- What strategies could make it harder for you to think about abusing someone again?

Situation clues

Signals

1. Being on my own with Tom.

2. Knowing my parents would be out for an hour at least.

3. Playing a game where I was touching Tom.

4. Putting rude pictures from the internet on the computer.

Strategies

1. Avoid being alone with younger children.

2. Do not agree to look after younger children (how could I arrange this?).

3. Avoid playing games with children younger than me.

4. Never discuss sexual material to children or show it to them.

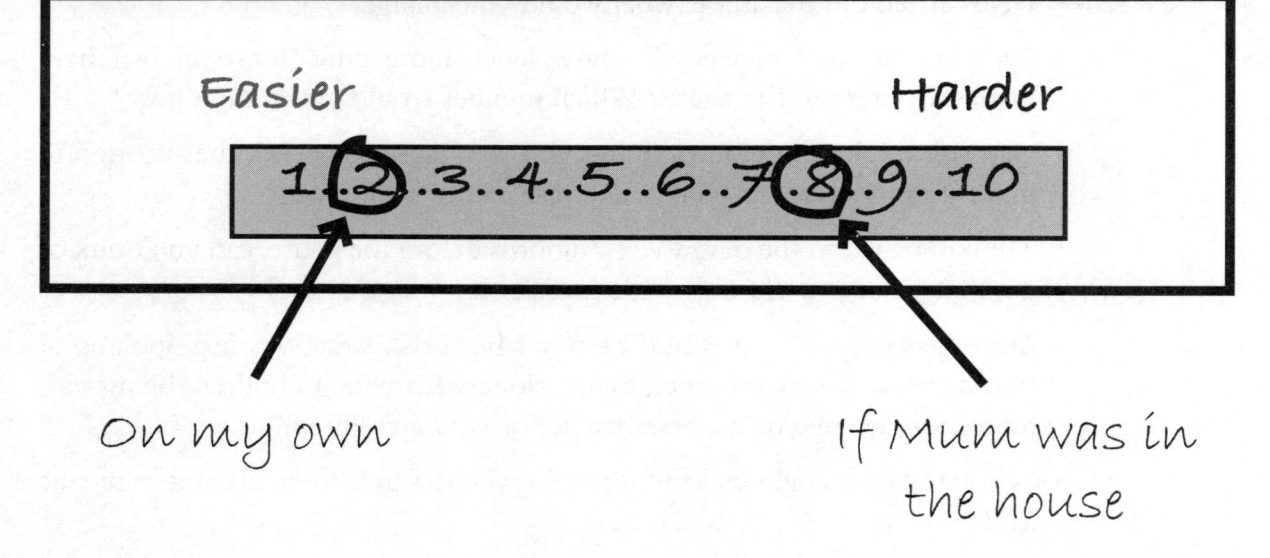

Easier   Harder

1..(2)..3..4..5..6..7..(8)..9..10

On my own   If Mum was in the house

Situation clues, worked example

Thought clues

Move on to explore the thoughts the YP had before their HSB. Draw up a new signals and strategies table, marking it 'Thought clues'. This is again with the aim of both identifying thoughts (and thought patterns) as well as thinking about strategies (or responses) to deal with those thoughts in order to reduce the likelihood of the YP acting out in a sexually abusive way. Some useful questions to ask include:

- When we explored the timeline before, we wrote down the thought you had just before you abused [*victim*]. [Read thought.] Can you remember what you were thinking before that? Think back to the thought you had just before that.
- What other thoughts seemed to pop into your head?
- What were the things that were going round in your head?
- Can you think of any thoughts you had that made it easier for you to decide to go ahead?
- What thoughts did you have before it happened about:
    - your victim?
    - yourself?
    - anybody else/[*name significant people*]?
    - life?
- Were there any fears going round in your head beforehand? What were they about? How did you try to deal with that fear?
- What were the things you were imagining might happen? Can you think back to any images that came up for you? How did you handle those images?
- In that moment, what were you hoping might happen?
- In that moment, what were you hoping you might feel? How did you try and make your hope come true?
- What thought made it easiest for you to abuse [*victim*]? What is wrong with these kind of (distorted) thoughts? How easy did it make it on a scale from 1–10? [Circle.]

Moving further back

The questions above can be used to explore thoughts at different points beforehand – you can ask the questions with reference to the minute before, hour before, day before and so on. Questions exploring further back include:

- When did you first start to think about [*victim*] in a sexual way?
- How did you deal with those thoughts when you first had them?
    - Did that lead to them getting better or worse?

Thought clues

Signals

1. 'He wanted it to happen'
2. 'He seems not to mind'
3. 'He hasn't said no'
4. 'This isn't hurting anyone. It's just a game'
5. 'Other people have done this to me'
6. 'This will show my step-dad'
7. 'Nobody cares about me'
8. 'I didn't plan to do this'
9. 'It is only one time'

Strategies
(example thought responses)

1. This person cannot give consent
2. A child does not know how damaging this can be
3. They are not able to understand this
4. This is hurting someone very badly
5. I still need to take responsibility for my actions
6. It is wrong to hurt other people
7. This will make it even harder for people to care for me
8. I am 100% responsible for my own actions
9. One time is enough to ruin someone's life

Easier 1..2..3..4..5..6..7..8..9..10 Harder

He wanted it to happen

A child cannot give consent – this will ruin his life

Thought clues, worked example

- How did your thoughts about [*victim*] grow over time?
- How did your thoughts about [*victim*] change over time?
- When you listened to those thoughts, did that help them to grow in your mind or stay away?

Here are some questions that can help to elicit strategies for the YP to use:

- Can you think of how you could have answered back to some of these thoughts?
- Are there times in the past when you have answered back to those thoughts and not abused someone?
  - What did you say?
  - What helped you listen to that thought?
  - What happened next?
- If a risky thought came into your head again, what would that tell you?
- What would you need to do?
- What would you say to answer the risky thought?
- What are the ways of dealing with your sexual thoughts about [children] that you'd like to keep with you for the future? That you'd like to make more use of?
- If you used this strategy and answered your thoughts back in this way – how much harder would it have been for you to abuse [*victim*]?

Feeling clues

Explore the YP's feelings before the abuse in a similar fashion. For the sake of simplicity the term 'feelings' is used here to refer to both emotions and physical sensations (such as sexual arousal). Questions may include:

- What feelings did you notice you had just before you started abusing [*victim*]?
  - Where did you notice that feeling in your body?
  - What did you think about that feeling?
  - What helped to make that feeling grow?
  - How did you deal with it?
  - Did that feeling make it easier or harder for you to abuse [*victim*]?
- Were you aware of any other feelings? In your body? In your mind? [Explore each as with the initial question above.]
- You mentioned you felt very angry, as well as a bit scared. Are you aware of feeling anything pleasant at all? Any slightly good feelings?
- Just before abusing [*victim*], how powerful/turned on/lonely/excited/loving/scared were you feeling? [Explore as above.]

- What feeling(s) made it easiest for you to abuse [*victim*]? How easy did your feeling make it easy on a scale from 1–10 to abuse your victim? [Circle.]

It is also important to acknowledge if the YP was sexually aroused and if this felt good to them. It can be important to actually state whether they were physically aroused ('*Was your penis hard?*') as this is a clear signal of their sexually aroused state.

Moving further back

The questions above can be used to explore feelings at different points beforehand – the therapist can ask the questions with reference to the minute before, hour before, day before and so on. Questions exploring further back include:

- When did you first start to have sexual feelings about [*victim*] [children]?
- How did you deal with those thoughts when you first had them? Did that lead to them getting weaker or stronger?
- How did your feelings about [*victim*] grow/change over time?
- Did anything happen to make your feelings stronger?

Here are some questions that can help to elicit strategies for the YP to use:

- Can you think of how you could have dealt with those feelings in a way that would not have hurt anyone?
- Are there times in the past when you have found other ways to deal with [*name feelings identified by the YP*]?
    - What did you do?
    - How did that help?
    - What happened next?
- If you had a strong feeling like this one again, what would that tell you?
- What would you need to do?
- What are the ways of dealing with your sexual feelings that you'd like to keep with you for the future? [Refer to those already covered.]
- If you dealt with your feelings using these strategies how much harder would it have been for you to abuse [*victim*]?

Some young people may minimise the existence of 'dangerous' thoughts and feelings before they abuse. They may state that nothing was going on for them. This helps to leave any thoughts unchallenged. If this occurs, it is often fruitful to explore with the YP who they think is more worrying: someone who has no warning signals that they might be likely to abuse, or someone who can spot warning signals. Explore with the YP their thoughts about each, drawing to the conclusion that identifying warning signals helps to lower risk, and gives both the YP and others around them confidence.

Appendix I: Sample Session Plans and Home Projects 135

Feeling clues

Signals

1. I felt angry

2. I felt sexually excited
3. Touching my willy felt good

4. I wanted to see what her privates felt like
5. My heart was racing

6. I wanted to come to make me feel good

Strategies

1. There are good ways to deal with anger – hurting others is wrong. Use my anger strategies
2. Have healthy sexual fantasies
3. Sex without consent is damaging and has serious consequences for me
4. Sit down and write out what my life will be like if I do this
5. It is hard to think clearly when I am excited like this – get out of the situation
6. I can masturbate in private

Easier   Harder

1..②..3..4..5..6..7..⑧..9..10

↑ Feeling angry and sexually excited

↑ Get out of the situation – write down the consequences for me

Feeling clues, worked example

4. ISSUES TO DISCUSS

Issues or incidents raised by the YP.

5. SUMMARY AND HOME PROJECT

Summarise the main points covered today. Explain that the home project provides an opportunity to draw together what you have learnt in today's session and record:

1. key warning signals
2. effective strategies to deal with them.

This can then be used by the YP in future to help spot dangerous situations and deal with them effectively. Praise the YP (as appropriate) for talking about difficult topics and use this as evidence of the progress the YP is making.

6. FEEDBACK

Obtain feedback in the usual way and bring the session to a close. '*How did you find today's session? Tell me one thing you thought was helpful, and one thing that was difficult.*'

HOME PROJECT 6:
KNOWING MY SIGNALS AND STRENGTHS

You have spent some time thinking about the different kinds of signals that you can spot which may make you more at risk of sexually harming someone. These signals are important clues that can allow you to change your thinking and your behaviour to keep yourself safe.

In the first part of this home project list the key situations, thoughts and feelings that have in the past increased (or might in the future increase) your risk of harming someone sexually. In the second part, summarise the key strategies that you can use to respond to these signals. These could be things you think or do. Try to remember the ideas discussed in your session.

MY SIGNALS

Situations

- _____
- _____
- _____
- _____

Thoughts

- _____
- _____
- _____
- _____

Feelings

- _____
- _____
- _____
- _____

MY STRATEGIES

To deal with my risky situations

- _____
- _____
- _____
- _____

To deal with my risky thoughts

- _____
- _____
- _____
- _____

To deal with my risky feelings

- _____
- _____
- _____
- _____

Road Map for the Future

Session 4: Staying in the Driving Seat

> **CORE AIMS**
>
> - To renew the young person's motivation to choose a positive future trajectory
> - To identify those 'driving seat' skills that will help them succeed
> - To identify the 'driving seat' skills that will help them avoid future harmful sexual behaviour.

OVERVIEW OF THE SESSION

This session takes a similar approach to that followed last week. The focus is to help the YP think how they could apply their learning from the Self-Regulation module to the same hypothetical situation. As in the previous session your goal is to help them elaborate their responses and prompt them where necessary in order to consolidate their strategies for relapse prevention.

1. WEEKLY REVIEW – SETTING THE AGENDA – HOME PROJECT

As usual, briefly review how the YP's week has been. Check if there are any issues that need to be brought back for discussion later in the session.

> *'Today we are going to spend some more time thinking about how what you have learnt can help you reach your goals and stay safe. We will be thinking back to the different skills we covered about staying in the driving seat. Does that sound okay?'*

> *Beginning*
>
> Review of the week – Home project
>
> *Main tasks*
>
> My timeline: Back to the future
>
> How my new driving seat skills can keep me safe
>
> *Ending*
>
> New home project – Issues to discuss – Feedback

'Is there anything you would like to discuss or add to the agenda this week?'

Review the YP's home project. Review with them which tools from the Relationships module they would find most helpful. Have they been using any of them already? If so, how have they worked? Have they come across any problems?

2. TIMELINE: BACK TO THE FUTURE

Review the YP's positive vision of the future

Explain that this week you are going to focus on what the YP learnt about being 'in the driving seat'. Either write up the key skills covered on the flip-chart or put an A3 copy of the list provided on the wall.

3. DRIVING SEAT SKILLS KEEPING ME SAFE

Recap the self-regulation toolkit

'Okay, let's start by reminding ourselves of the different skills you learnt from the 'In the driving seat' module'. These are:

1. Managing feelings
2. Anger strategies

Appendix I: Sample Session Plans and Home Projects 143

DRIVING SEAT TOOLKIT

🔧 Managing feelings

MONITOR FEELINGS — Situation, Feelings, Thoughts

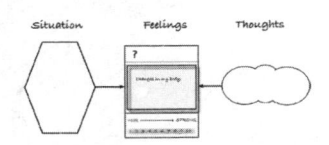

GET THE VOLUME RIGHT

DOWNSIDES OF AGGRESSION

🔧 Stragegies for sexually abusive feelings

ESCAPE	BE ASSERTIVE	TAKE CONTROL	SEEK SUPPORT	TIME OUT
SAFE PLACE	SAY NO!	POSITIVE STATEMENT CONSEQUENCES	PEOPLE I CAN TALK TO	SAFE ACTIVITIES

🔧 Anger strategies

BE ASSERTIVE	TIME OUT	RELAXATION	GETAWAY IMAGE	BIG PICTURE
ME-YOU-NEW	SAFE ACTIVITIES			

🔧 Making better choices EARLY – Taking responsibility

3. Strategies for sexually abusive feelings
4. Making better choices.

'You can think of these as different skills in your toolkit.'

Now shift the YP's focus to the hypothetical risk scenario developed last week. Ensure that the three scenes are placed on the wall in easy view. It may be simplest to put a clean sheet underneath each in order to create space for the YP to brainstorm about their self-regulation skills.

Again, ask the YP to identify the different strategies that they would find most useful to help them to successfully deal with this risk scenario. Ask them to list at least two for each scene and explain how these would help them.

Key tools covered in this module:

1. Managing feelings
   - Monitoring my feelings
   - Getting the volume right
   - Balanced thinking
   - Downsides of aggression
2. Anger strategies
   - Being assertive
   - Time out
   - Relaxation
   - My getaway image
   - The big picture
3. Strategies for sexually abusive feelings
   - Escape – avoid risky situations
   - Be assertive – say NO!
   - Take control and see the consequences
   - Seek support
   - Time out – distract yourself
4. Making better choices
   - Spotting clues to my HSB: situations, thoughts, feelings
   - Making the right choices early
   - Taking 100% responsibility for my actions.

The following questions should be used appropriately depending on the hypothetical scenario that the YP has created. Some may be useful to only one scene, while others may be relevant throughout. The aim is to encourage the YP to think actively *for themselves* about the different strategies that they have learnt and apply them to a new situation.

Questions for Step 1: Managing feelings

- What kind of feelings do you think you might have in this situation? How strong might they be?
- How would you first notice these feelings? How would your body feel different?
- How would these feelings make it difficult to make good choices?
- What kind of thoughts would help turn the volume down on your feelings?
- If you noticed yourself feeling like this what could you say to yourself? How would you fight back?
- How could you look after yourself when you have a feeling like that?
- Is there anyone that could help you/who you would want to talk to?
- What do you think would be the best thing that you could do to manage your feelings?

Questions for Step 2: Anger strategies

- How angry do you think you would be feeling (1–10)?
- What ways could you use to deal with your anger?
- Can you tell me a different way of looking at the situation that would make you feel better?
- What kind of anger strategies could you use? Can you tell me how you would use this?
- Which strategy do you think would work best here/what has worked best for you? Why?
- How would you go about putting it into practice?
- How could you act assertively in this situation? What would you do?

Questions for Step 3: Strategies for sexually abusive feelings

- How sexually aroused do you think you would be feeling (1–10)?
- How do you think that would affect your ability to make good choices?

- What ways could you use to deal with your sexual arousal?
- Can you tell me how you could deal with your sexual arousal in a different way?
- What kind of strategies could you use? Which one do you think would work best here?
- How would you go about putting it into practice?

Questions for Step 4: Making better choices

- What would be a poor choice?
- What would be a better choice you could make?
- Is there another choice you could have made earlier? Tell me about that. Would this have been easier or harder?
- What would help you make a better choice? What would make it harder?
- What kind of things could you do that would help you make a better choice?
- Can you think of a time when you were able to make a good choice like this in the past? How did you manage to do that?
- How responsible would you be if you abused Tony? Would it be fair to blame anyone else?
- Given that you would be 100% responsible for abusing Tony, how would you feel afterwards about yourself?

4. ISSUES TO DISCUSS

Issues or incidents raised by the YP.

5. SUMMARY AND HOME PROJECT

Summarise the main points covered today. Like last week praise the YP for their specific contributions to dealing with the hypothetical risk situation. Highlight any ways the YP has already shown evidence of using these skills and strategies. Make sure to check out your summary with the YP: '*Have I got that right? Is there anything you'd like to add?*' Explain that next week the YP will be able to take their home project file home with them to keep; check that they are happy for you to copy this file to keep as part of their clinical record.

Explain that the home project will require the YP to create another collage or picture story of themselves, similar to the one that they created in the second session. (Please see Home Project 2, part 2 from Session 2 in the Engagement Module). This picture should be called the 'New Me' and include the new skills, knowledge and confidence that the YP now feels.

6. FEEDBACK

Obtain feedback in the usual way and bring the session to a close. '*How did you find today's session? Tell me one thing you thought was helpful, and one thing that was difficult.*'

Appendix II

Samples from the Character Library Material

Appendix II: Samples from the Character Library Material   151

References

Achenbach, T. (1991) *Manual for the Youth Self-Report and 1991 Profile.* Burlington: University of Vermont, Department of Psychology.

Achenbach, T. and Edelbrock, C. (1991) *Manual for the Child Behavior Checklist and Revised Child Behavior Profile.* Burlington: University of Vermont, Department of Psychology.

Ackerman, S. and Hilsenroth, M. (2003) 'A Review of Therapist Characteristics and Techniques Positively Impacting the Therapeutic Alliance.' *Clinical Psychology Review* 23, 1–33.

Ayland, L. and West, B. (2006) 'The Good Way model: A Strengths-based Approach for Working with Young People, Especially Those with Intellectual Disabilities, who have Sexually Abusive Behaviour.' *Journal of Sexual Aggression* 12, 189–201.

Barbaree, H.E. and Marshall, W.L. (eds) (2005) *The Juvenile Sex Offender* (2nd edn). London: Guilford Press.

Beck, A.T. (1979) *Cognitive Treatment and the Emotional Disorders.* New York: Meridian.

Beck, J.S. (1995) *Cognitive Therapy: Basics and Beyond.* New York: Guilford Press.

Beech, A.R., Fisher, D.D. and Thornton, D. (2003) 'Risk Assessment of Sex Offenders.' *Professional Psychology: Research and Practice* 34, 4, 339–352.

Bentovim, A. (1995) *Trauma Organized Systems: Physical and Sexual Abuse in Families.* London and New York: Karnac.

Bentovim, A. (2004) 'Working with Abusing Families: General Issues and a Systemic Perspective.' *Journal of Family Psychotherapy* 15, 1, 119–135.

Blanchard, R., Watson, M., Choy, A., Dickey, R., Klassen, P., Kuban, N. and Feren, D.J. (1999) 'Paedophiles: Mental Retardation, Maternal Age and Sexual Orientation.' *Archives of Sexual Behaviour* 28, 111–127.

Bowlby, J. (1969) *Attachment and Loss, Vol 1. Attachment* (2nd edn). New York: Basic Books.

Briere, J. (1996) *Trauma Symptom Checklist for Children (TSCC).* Odessa, FL: Psychological Assessment Resources.

Brooks-Gordon, B., Bilby, C. and Wells, H. (2006) 'A Systematic Review of Psychological Interventions of Sexual Offenders I: Randomised Control Trials.' *Journal of Forensic Psychiatry and Psychology* 17, 3, 442–466.

Burton, D., Miller, D. and Shill, C.T. (2002) 'A Social Learning Theory Comparison of the Sexual Victimization of Adolescent Sexual Offenders and Non-sexual Offending Male Delinquents.' *Child Abuse and Neglect* 26, 893–907.

Butler, S.M. and Seto, M.C. (2002) 'Distinguishing Two Types of Adolescent Sex Offenders.' *Journal of the American Academy of Child and Adolescent Psychiatry* 41, 83–90.

Craig, L. and Hutchinson, R.B. (2005) 'Sexual Offenders with Learning Disabilities: Risk, Recidivism and Treatment.' *Journal of Sexual Aggression* 11, 289–304.

Department for Children, Schools and Families (DCSF) (2010) *Working Together to Safeguard Children: A Guide to Inter-agency Working to Safeguard and Promote the Welfare of Children.* London: DCSF. Downloadable at: http://publications.dcsf.gov.uk/default.aspx?PageFunction=productdetails&PageMode=publications&ProductId=DCSF-00305-2010

Department of Health (2001) *Valuing People: A New Strategy for Learning Disability for the 21st Century.* London: Department of Health.

Department of Health (Health Care Partnerships Directorate and Home Office: Youth Justice and Children Team) (2006) *The Needs and Effective Treatment of Young People who Sexually Abuse: Current Evidence.* London: Department of Health.

Eltz, M.J., Shirk, S. and Sarlin, N. (1995) 'Alliance Formation and Treatment Outcome among Maltreated Adolescents.' *Child Abuse and Neglect* 19, 419–431.

Erikson, E.H. (1959/1980) *Identity and the Life Cycle.* New York: Norton.

Fonagy, P., Gergely, G., Jurist, E.J., Target, M. (2002) *Affect Regulation, Mentalization and the Development of the Self.* New York: Other Press.

Fonagy, P., Target, M., Cottrell, D., Phillips, J. and Kurtz, Z. (2005).' *What Works for Whom? A Critical Review of Treatments for Children and Adolescents.* New York: Guilford Press.

Forth, A.E., Kosson, D.S. and Hare, R.D. (2003) *Hare PCL: Youth Version. Technical Manual.* North Tonawanda, NY: Multi-Health Systems (MHS).

Fortune, C. and Lambie, I. (2004) 'Demographic and Abuse Characteristics in Adolescent Male Sexual Offenders with "Special Needs." *Journal of Sexual Aggression* 10, 63–84.

Friedrich, W.N., Lysne, M., Sim, L. and Shamos, S. (2004) 'Assessing Sexual Behavior in High-risk Adolescents with the Adolescent Clinical Sexual Behavior Inventory'. *Child Maltreatment* 9, 3, 239–250.

Goodman, R. (1997) 'The Strengths and Difficulties Questionnaire: A Research Note.' *Journal of Child Psychology and Psychiatry* 38, 581–586.

Griffin, H. and Beech, A. (2004) *Evaluation of the AIM Framework for Assessment of Adolescents who Display Sexually Harmful Behaviour.* London: Youth Justice Board.

Hackett, S. (2004) *What Works for Children and Young People with Harmful Sexual Behaviours.* Essex: Barnardo's.

Hackett, S., Masson, H. and Phillips, S. (2003) *Mapping and Exploring Services for Young People who have Sexually Abused Others.* A two-year research project funded by Youth Justice Board, NSPCC and The National Organisation for the Treatment of Abusers. University of Durham and University of Huddersfield: Centre for Applied Social and Community Studies, and the Centre for Applied Childhood Studies.

Hackett, S., Masson, H. and Phillips, S. (2006) 'Exploring Consensus in Practice with Youth who are Sexually Abusive: Findings from a Delphi Study of Practitioner Views in the United Kingdom and the Republic of Ireland.' *Child Maltreatment* 11, 2, 146–156.

Hawkes, C. (2002) 'Accreditation of Work and Workers Involved in Providing a Service to Children and Young People who Sexually Abuse.' In Martin C. Calder (ed.) *Young People who Sexually Abuse.* Lyme Regis: Russell House Publishing, Dorset.

Hetherton, J. (1999) 'The Idealization of Women: Its Role in the Minimization of Child Sexual Abuse by Females.' *Child Abuse and Neglect* 23, 161–174.

Hickey, N., McCrory, E., Farmer, E., Vizard, E. (2008) 'Comparing the Developmental and Behavioural Characteristics of Female and Male Juveniles who Present with Sexually Abusive Behaviour.' *Journal of Sexual Aggression* 14, 3, 241–252.

Hickey, N., Vizard, E., French, L., McCrory, E. (2006) *Links between Juvenile Sexually Abusive Behaviour and Emerging Severe Personality Disorder Traits.* London: Department of Health. www.dh.gov.uk

Home Office (2003) *Criminal Statistics: England and Wales 2002. Statistics Relating to Criminal Proceedings for the Year 2002.* London: The Stationery Office.

Kavoussi, R.J., Kaplan, M. and Becker, J.V. (1988) 'Psychiatric Diagnoses in Adolescent Sexual Offenders.' *Journal of the American Academy of Child and Adolescent Psychiatry* 27, 241–243.

Lader, D., Singleton, N. and Meltzer, H. (2003) 'Psychiatric Morbidity among Young Offenders in England and Wales.' *International Review of Psychiatry* 15, 144–147.

Lambert, M.J. (1992) 'Implications of Outcome Research for Psychotherapy Integration.' In J.C. Norcross and M.R. Goldstein (eds) *Handbook of Psychotherapy Integration*. New York: John Wiley and Sons.

Lindsay, W.R., Elliott, S.F. and Astell, A. (2004) 'Predictors of Sexual Offence Recidivism in Offenders with Intellectual Disabilities.' *Journal of Applied Research in Intellectual Disabilities* 17, 299–305

Lindsay, W. (2005) 'Model underpinning treatment for sex offenders with mild intellectual disability: Current theories of sex offending.' *Mental Retardation 43*, 428–441.

Littell, J., Popa, M. and Forsythe, B. (2005) *Multisystemic Therapy for Social, Emotional and Behavioural Problems in Youth Aged 10–17*. Cochrane Database Systematic Review CD004797.

Losel, F. and Schmucker, M. (2005) 'The Effectiveness of Treatment for Sexual Offenders: A Comprehensive Meta-analysis.' *Journal of Experimental Criminology* 1, 117–146.

MacKenzie, D. (2006) *What Works in Corrections – Reducing the Criminal Activities of Offenders and Delinquents*. Cambridge: Cambridge University Press.

Marshall, W.L. (2005) 'Therapist Style in Sexual Offender Treatment: Influence on Indices of Change'. *Sexual Abuse: A Journal of Research and Treatment* 17, 109–116.

Mathews, R., Hunter, J. and Vuz, J. (1997) 'Juvenile Female Sexual Offenders: Clinical Characteristics and Treatment Issues.' *Sexual Abuse: A Journal of Research and Treatment* 9, 187–199.

McCrory, E. and Farmer, E. (2009) 'Effective Psychological Interventions for Conduct Problems: Current Evidence and New Directions' In S. Hodgins, E., Viding and A. Plodowski (eds) *Persistent Violent Offenders: Neuroscience And Rehabilitation*. (1st edn) Oxford: Oxford University Press.

McCrory, E., Hickey, N., Farmer, E. and Vizard, E. (2008) 'Early-Onset Sexually Harmful Behaviour in Childhood: A Marker for Life Course Persistent Antisocial Behaviour?' *British Journal of Forensic Psychiatry and Psychology* 19, 3, 382–395.

McMackin, R.A., Leisen, M.B., Cusack, J.F., Lafratta, J. and Litwin, P. (2002) 'The Relationship of Trauma Exposure to Sex Offending Behavior among Male Juvenile Offenders.' *Journal of Child Sexual Abuse* 11, 25–40.

Miccio-Fonseca, L. (2009) 'MEGA: A New Paradigm in Protocol Assessing Sexually Abusive Children and Adolescents.' *Journal of Child and Adolescent Trauma* 2, 2, 124–141.

Miller, W.R. and Rollnick, S. (2002) *Motivational Interviewing: Preparing People to Change Addictive Behaviour* (2nd edn). New York: Guilford Press.

Moffitt, T.E. (1993) 'Adolescence Limited and Life Course Persistent Antisocial Behaviour: A Developmental Taxonomy.' *Psychological Review* 100, 674–701.

Moffitt, T.E. (2006) 'Life-course Persistent versus Adolescence-limited Antisocial Behaviour.' In D. Cicchetti and D. Cohen (eds) *Developmental Psychopathology, Vol. 3: Risk, Disorder, and Adaptation* (2nd edn). New York: Wiley.

Moffitt, T. and Caspi, A. (2001) 'Childhood Predictors Differentiate Life-course Persistent and Adolescence-limited Antisocial Pathways among Males and Females.' *Development and Psychopathology* 13, 355–375.

National Task Force on Juvenile Sexual Offending (1993) 'The Revised Report on Juvenile Sexual Offending 1993 of the National Adolescent Perpetration Network.' *Juvenile and Family Court Journal* 44, 1–120.

O'Brien, M.J. and Bera, W. (1986) 'Adolescent Sexual Offenders: A Descriptive Typology.' *Preventing Sexual Abuse* 1, 3, 1–4.

O'Callaghan, D. (1998) 'Practice Issues in Working with Young Abusers who have Learning Disabilities.' *Child Abuse Review* 7, 435–448.

Ochsner, K.N. and Gross, J.J. (2005) 'The Cognitive Control of Emotion.' *Trends in Cognitive Science* 9, 5, 242–249.

Parry, C. and Lindsay, W.R. (2003) 'Impulsiveness as a Factor in Sexual Offending by People with Mild Intellectual Disability.' *Journal of Intellectual Disability Research* 47, 483–487.

Prentky, R.A., Harris, B., Frizzell, K. and Righthand, S. (2000) 'An Actuarial Procedure for Assessing Risk with Juvenile Sex Offenders.' *Sexual Abuse: A Journal of Research and Treatment* 12, 71–93.

Print, B., Morrison, T. and Henniker, J. (2001) 'An Inter-agency Assessment Framework for Young People who Sexually Abuse: Principles, Processes and Practicalities.' In M.C. Calder (ed.) *Juveniles and Children who Sexually Abuse: Frameworks for Assessment*. Lyme Regis: Russell House Publishing.

Prochaska, J.O. and DiClemente, C.C. (1992) *Stages of Change in the Modification of Problem Behaviors*. Newbury Park, CA: Sage

Reitzel, L. and Carbonell, J. (2006) 'The Effectiveness of Sexual Offender Treatment for Juveniles as Measured by Recidivism: A Meta-Analysis.' *Sex Abuse* 18, 401–421.

Rich, P. (2003) *Understanding, Assessing and Rehabilitating Juvenile Sexual Offenders*. Hoboken, NJ: John Wiley and Sons, Inc.

Rich, P. (2006) *Attachment and Sexual Offending: Understanding and Applying Attachment Theory to the Treatment of Juvenile Sexual Offenders*. Chichester: John Wiley and Sons Ltd.

Rich, P. (2009) *Juvenile Sexual Offenders: A Comprehensive Guide to Risk Evaluation*. Chichester: John Wiley and Sons Ltd.

Riggs, N.R., Greenberg, M.T., Kusché, C.A. and Pentz, M.A. (2006) 'The Mediational Role of Neurocognition in the Behavioral Outcomes of a Social-emotional Prevention Program in Elementary School Students: Effects of the PATHS Curriculum.' *Prevention Science* 7, 1, 91–102.

Righthand, S. and Welch, C. (2004) 'Characteristics of Youths who Sexually Offend.' *Journal of Child Sexual Abuse* 13, 15–32.

Righthand, S., Prentky, R., Knight, R., Carpenter, E., Hecker, J.E. and Nangle, D. (2005) 'Factor Structure and Validation of the Juvenile Sex Offender Assessment Protocol (J-SOAP).' *Sexual Abuse: A Journal of Research and Treatment* 17, 1, 13–30.

Rosenberg, M. (1965) *Society and the Adolescent Self-image*. Princeton, NJ: Princeton University Press.

Salter, D., McMillan, D., Richards, M., Talbot, T., Hodges, J., Bentovim, A., Hastings, R., Stevenson, J. and Skuse, D. (2003) 'Development of Sexually Abusive Behaviour in Sexually Abused Males: A Longitudinal Study.' *Lancet* 361, 471–476.

Sefarbi, R. (1990) 'Admitters and Deniers among Adolescent Sex Offenders and their Families: A Preliminary Study.' *American Journal of Orthopsychiatry* 60, 460–465.

Snyder, H. (2005) *Juvenile Arrests 2003*. US Office of Juvenile Justice and Delinquency Prevention. Available at: www.ncjrs.gov/pdffiles1/ojjdp/209735.pdf (accessed 3 July 2009).

Steinberg, L. (2005) 'Cognitive and Affective Development in Adolescence.' *Trends in Cognitive Sciences* 9, 2, 69–74.

Taylor, J.F. (2003) 'Children and Young People Accused of Child Sexual Abuse: A Study within a Community.' *Journal of Sexual Aggression* 9, 57–70.

Thakker, J., Ward, T. and Tidmarsh, P. (2006) 'A Re-evalution of Relapse Prevention with Adolescents who Sexually Offend: A Good Lives Model.' In H.E. Barbaree and W.L. Marshall (eds) *The Juvenile Sex Offender* (2nd edn). London: Guilford Press.

van Wijk, A.P., Vermeiren, R., Loeber, R., Hart-Kerkhoffs, L., Doreleijers, T. and Bullens, R. (2006) 'Juvenile Sex Offenders Compared to Non-sex Offenders: A Review of the Literature 1995–2005.' *Trauma, Violence and Abuse* 7, 4, 227–243.

Vizard, E. (2002) 'The Assessment of Young Sexual Abusers.' In M.C. Calder (ed.) *Young People who Sexually Abuse* Lyme Regis: Russell House Publishing.

Vizard, E., Hickey, N., French, L. and McCrory, E. (2007a) 'Children and Adolescents who Present with Sexually Abusive Behaviour: A UK Descriptive Study.' *Journal of Forensic Psychiatry and Psychology* 18, 1, 59–73.

Vizard, E., Hickey, N. McCrory, E. (2007b) 'Developmental trajectories Associated with Juvenile Sexually Abusive Behaviour and Emerging Severe Personality Disorder in Childhood: The Results of a Three Year UK study. *British Journal of Psychiatry* 190, s27–s32.

Vizard, E., Wynick, S., Hawkes, C., Woods, J. and Jenkins, J. (1996) 'Juvenile Sexual Offenders: Assessment Issues.' *British Journal of Psychiatry* 3, 259–262.

Walker, D.F., McGovern, S.K., Poey, E.L. and Otis, K.E. (2004) 'Treatment Effectiveness for Male Adolescent Sexual Offenders: A Meta-analysis and Review.' *Journal of Child Sexual Abuse* 13, 281–293.

Wieckowski, E., Hartsoe, P., Mayer, A. and Shortz, J. (1998) 'Deviant Sexual Behaviour in Children and Young Adolescents: Frequency and Patterns.' *Sexual Abuse: A Journal of Research and Treatment* 10, 293–303.

Worling, J.R. (2004) 'The Estimate of Risk of Adolescent Sexual Offense Recidivism (ERASOR): Preliminary Psychometric Data.' *Sexual Abuse: Journal of Research and Treatment* 16, 235–254.

Worling, J.R. and Curwen, T. (2000) 'Adolescent Sexual Offender Recidivism: Success of Specialised Treatment and Implications for Risk Prediction.' *Child Abuse and Neglect* 24, 7, 965–982.

Worling, J.R. and Curwen, T. (2001) 'The "ERASOR" Estimate of Risk of Adolescent Sexual Offense Recidivism.' In M.C. Calder (ed.) *Juveniles and Children who Sexually Abuse: Frameworks for Assessment.* Lyme Regis: Russell House Publishing.

Youth Justice Board (2006) *Asset – Young Offender Assessment Profile (2006 Edition).* London: Youth Justice Board. www.yjb.gov.uk

Youth Justice Board (2008) *Assessment, Planning, Interventions and Supervision.* London: Youth Justice Board. www.yjb.gov.uk